How to Create
POSITIVE
Relationships
with Students

A Handbook
of Group Activities
and Teaching
Strategies

Michelle Karns

WITH CONTRIBUTIONS FROM
Emily Garfield, Steve Zuieback,
and Lorna Cunkle

Research Press   2612 North Mattis Avenue   Champaign, Illinois 61821

Cover design by Linda Brown
Illustrations by Kitty Wright
Composition by TBH/Typecast, Inc.
Printed by Malloy Lithographing

ISBN 0–87822–348–7
Library of Congress Catalog No. 94–66557

For Wayne and Nancy:

I am grateful for your trust and belief in me.
I can never truly express my gratitude
for the opportunities shared and the dreams realized.
I am appreciative—you have made a difference in my life.

For Steve:

It is sometimes tough to be a good friend. Thanks.

For Kitty:

I have only admiration and respect for your talent,
commitment, and open heart.

For Robert:

I will never be able to describe how I value your support.
You strive to be the best and challenge me to do the same.
Thanks for the back rubs and the late-night laughter.
Thanks for always believing that I could write a book
and for doing all the vacuuming.

For Katy,
the person for whom this book has been written:

I wish you many adult mentors and guides.

For all the dreams and memories made
outside our home by caring folks:

I am grateful.

Contents

Foreword

THIS HANDBOOK IS A TANTALIZING COLLECTION of Michelle Karns'
magic for use by parents, teachers, and others working directly with
children of all ages, but in particular with preadolescent and adolescent
age groups. In these pages she introduces us to her wonderful repertoire
of games and activities that so captivate her youthful audiences. With
these ideas, you too can teach new skills and self-understanding, and the
kids will have fun while learning.

The activities here also provide us with some keys to inter- and
intragenerational connectivity. Play becomes an opportunity to open
communication windows—child to child, child to adult, adult to child,
and group to group.

I think you will find this handbook intriguing, enchanting, sur-
prising, and challenging. You will quickly find it indispensable as you
use it to communicate more productively with the young people in your
life. Select the activities that seem appropriate for you and those with
which you feel comfortable. Try them with your own family or a small
group before using them with larger audiences. Let us know how it goes
for you and if you find other ways of accomplishing the same aims with a
different approach.

—*Emily Garfield, Ph.D.*
Senior Staff Associate
National Training Associates

Preface

I AM CONVINCED THAT ANYONE, armed with good skills and strategies, can be effective with kids. While some folks find it easier than others, the truth is that anybody who wants to make a difference in a kid's life can. The recipe is pretty simple: three parts "wanting" and two parts "willing."

Emily Garfield and Steve Zuieback gave me more "wanting" and "willing" than any others. They were great cheerleaders, convincing me that I know some things worth sharing. They advised me, wrote with me, edited me, and laughed with me.

This handbook, full of memories that I hold important, is a synthesis of my career working with kids. In some ways, it is my cathartic project since I "recovered" from being a therapist and became a teacher. In other ways, it is everything I wish I had known before I started working with kids. My hope is that you will find the information and activities presented here to be valuable and worthwhile.

My work with kids has been fun, and memories continue to frame my desire and willingness to work with kids. I remember . . .

> . . . a young woman who first gave me a window to understand "letting go." After two years as an addict and a prostitute, she chose to become clean and sober. She said that letting go "was giving herself the power to give up the pain." She also said she would never forget her time on the streets—she could only forgive herself and move on. Great lessons. I wish I could recount all the times her wisdom helped someone else.

> . . . that special kid, Billy, who let me know in no uncertain terms that most adults are stupid. Stupid? "Yes," said he, "adults are stupid because they always think they know stuff that they couldn't possibly know— like how I feel and what it is like to have stuff happen." His definition of "stupid" describes how I approached kids in the past: "I am the expert—let me tell you what to do." Now my strategy is very different: "What's happening?" "How are you handling it now?" "What is working?" "Help me know what you need from me." A *very* different approach. Thanks, Billy.

. . . an old man named Pete who gave me some great advice. "You see," he said, "Parents have a very specific job: to plan and prepare kids for the big picnic—life. Every kid gets a picnic basket at birth. Parents and family are charged with the duty of filling the picnic basket. When kids are infants and toddlers, they almost totally rely on the picnic baskets supplied by their parents. As they grow up, they become more and more self-reliant and begin to fill their own baskets. Sometimes people get lost on their journey, and then their recovery is to repack their picnic baskets." Listening, I quipped, "All I bring to the picnic is the ants." Pete quietly nodded and said, "Well, it wouldn't be a picnic without some ants."

While many have left marks on how and who I am, no one has had a greater impact on my life than my own daughter, Katy. From her I have been challenged to question the essence of life itself. Not a day goes by that I don't check my gratitude for her laughter, hugs, and daily dialogues. I remember . . .

. . . Katy as a toddler. I tried to potty train her early so my mother would be impressed with my great skill. I took Katy into the bathroom several times a day, and we sat and read and laughed. She never did her "duty," but I knew the time would come when she would respond. She did. My mother came to visit. She brought Katy books. Katy went to the bathroom to read. I trained her well—to read in the bathroom.

My daughter keeps me humble. She has helped me to understand what Jean Piaget meant when he said that you only have to observe a child to witness a miracle.

But why tell you these stories? It is simple, really. These memories help me get through my everyday life with my daughter and all the other kids I meet. By conjuring the memories and reliving them, I find it easier to reach out to anybody's kid. Maybe it's an idea to try.

Somehow, my hope is that you will take on some responsibility to reach out to someone else's child. I am convinced that we must work together to effect positive change for children. I try to live by an African proverb made popular by Alex Haley: "It takes the whole village to raise a child." Perhaps this proverb fits for you?

—*Michelle Karns*
November 1993
Davis, California

PART I

On Being a Valuable Adult

CHAPTER 1
Communicating with Kids

MOST ADULTS HAVE PROBLEMS at some time communicating with kids. The reasons vary. Some difficulty may be attributed to unspoken expectations. Others have problems because they misread maturity and are not age appropriate in their interactions. Still others have problems because they assume understanding and fail to check their perceptions.

Most communication errors are a product of time—not taking the time to check for understanding and verification that the message was clear. The sender of the message is responsible for clarity and, ultimately, the success of the communication. Somehow, when it comes to kids and their communication with adults, the kids are blamed for unsuccessful dialogue: "That kid doesn't listen. I could talk until I am blue in the face . . . I had his brother last year, and he was the same. These kids just don't . . ."

The kids are not always at fault. More often, adults do not know how to be heard! We have got to stop blaming the victims for being victimized. Too often, kids are burdened with labels and negative assumptions because the adults are unable to reach the child. Something is faulty in our logic. We are the professionals—the adults—and should strive to reach all children.

The beliefs that serve as the foundation of my work with kids are simple but direct:

All kids can learn, but not in the same way at the same time.

It is my job to discern strategies that will meet the kids where they are rather than where it could be convenient for me to have them be.

All kids need caring adults, and not all children are dealt them.

I have a responsibility as an educator to reach out to kids. I can provide an anchor to a child needing a positive perspective.

All kids need positive experiences in school, and grades are not necessarily the only way to measure school success.

In my life, humor, good friends, and a desire to learn have been more helpful than knowing the facts related to any specific subject. I strive to provide opportunities for student success in every interaction, an approach that I believe can override negative experiences that kids bring with them to school.

All kids need to be able to think, not just problem solve or state facts.

The two most important attributes of a successful human are:

1. the ability to think and to live life with the conviction of one's thoughts

2. the ability to communicate one's thoughts so that another understands them as was intended

All of these beliefs rely on the ability to communicate effectively in a time when communication is thwarted more often than supported. As the world has experienced rapid change, our abilities to develop relationships and to communicate with one another have been challenged.

In this fast-paced, immediately gratifying, adult-centered world, kids are being left out. Work demands have become central to family life. The family rules and roles have changed, too. Historically, the child-adult relationship was overlaid with social expectations and norms. These norms helped to frame behavior and set boundaries. Adults were elders, to be respected and revered. Kids were to be seen and not heard.

When Sister Edwarda came into my classroom, we stood and acknowledged her presence with "Good morning, Sister." She would respond, "Good morning, boys and girls," and that was the end of the dialogue. For the rest of the day she would talk *at* us. Like most of the adults in my life, my teachers used their role power to control and discipline.

As the world has turned during these last twenty years, inherent role power has eroded. Adults are being forced to face the fact that they no longer can use their power over kids as a means to get them to "do." Relationships are no longer a consequence of the roles played. Good relationships with kids are earned.

The best way to earn a relationship with a child is to gain his or her respect because of expertise, empathy, or effort. More often, influence is motivated by fear or reward. These forms of influence work for a short time, then gradually become more and more ineffective. Our best shot with children relies on our ability to be genuine and honest.

As adults we are all having to look at ourselves critically: What do I bring to the adult-kid relationship? Am I capable of having a relationship with a child that is nurturing and caring? The resiliency research (see chapter 3) reinforces the theory that the survival of children who live in adverse conditions is contingent upon successful relationships with adults. Being an adult in kids' lives makes a difference! We have much to overcome.

Somehow, the kid-adult relationship has become antagonistic. "We"—the adults—have to get "them"—the kids—to *do* something. The more "they" do not want to do what "we" want, the more rigid and restrictive the interaction. The more problematic the communication becomes, the fewer the attempts to have a real dialogue. I have kids in my life who report that the only time their parents talk with them is to complain about the condition of their rooms, criticize their choices, or inquire about the status of their homework. To paraphrase H. Stephen Glenn and Jane Nelsen: Kids have fewer than ten minutes a day with adults when they are not ordered, directed, or commanded.[1]

Ten minutes is far too little time. Kids can't possibly grow up secure, safe, and competent with so little time dedicated to their successful maturation. After a while, kids find it easier to eliminate interaction with adults than to cope with them. Bad choice: Eliminating adults from their lives slows kids' maturation, disenfranchises them from society's mainstream, and perpetuates the "we-they" myth.

I used to assume that what I had to say was central to my success as an adult-child communicator. I have come to believe that the primary experience of communication begins with the sense of relationship. For example, when I have rapport with a kid and say, "Try again— you missed a step," the preexisting relationship helps to frame the intent of my words. Using the same statement with a student with whom I have no rapport may communicate a totally different message.

How is rapport developed? It begins with an initial attraction. Think about it. The folks you are most attracted to bring something to the relationship that you need: Humor. Hope. A willingness to try. The ability to listen. Laughter. Something attractive. From attraction, the opportunity for rapport is established. To use the metaphor of a dance, rapport is being in step with someone—separate but together, sharing a common experience.

Within the context of rapport, permission is gleaned. Permission. Consent. Authority. This dimension of a relationship provides depth and intimacy. Permission to talk about feelings. Permission to ask for explanation. Permission to ask for help. Permission to be out of control. Permission to be real.

Experiencing attraction, rapport, and permission contributes to the next level of a relationship: influence. A relationship of influence is a connection that helps to "do," to be productive. The task is less relevant than doing it with someone of influence. Influence brings meaning to the connection. It serves to bridge the gaps between people.

Bridging the gaps—the generation gap and the communication gap—requires that you do more than talk. Your relationship building needs to be multidimensional, incorporating varied experiences. You already have opportunities to connect with kids in meaningful ways. *Doing* is the key.

If you want influential relationships with kids, you cannot be passive. One of the most common mistakes in adult-child liaisons is expecting intimacy because of the role you perceive yourself as playing in a kid's life. Do not assume that your role will inherently guarantee an important and viable connection. If you want to make a difference with kids, then you must be an active part of their lives.

Building a meaningful relationship requires your willingness to be vulnerable. This does not mean that you should burden kids with your secrets or your pain. In fact, you'll know that you have overstepped your limits when the kids turn the table on you and try to help you take care of your problems.

Your vulnerability should be restricted to the affective-feeling domain—the part of you that responds emotionally. What is important is not how you think about feelings but how you experience feelings. Often folks get confused. We have very few good teachers in this arena. Besides, we keep changing the rules.

In the sixties, we were supposed to "go with the feeling," but I didn't know where to go. In the seventies, it was hip to "talk about our feelings," but that usually ended up with me yelling; somehow, while talking my feelings "through," I got angry. Now, in the nineties, we need to express ourselves emotionally. Hidden in this challenge is the assumption that I know how to express myself emotionally.

I have learned what "emotional expression" means, but I still cannot do it without some guidance. Stated simply, the expression of feelings is the labeling of your experience with a term that you understand represents the experience. Sharing your feeling experiences with others without rationalizing or setting conditions leads to vulnerability.

Using the language of feelings will help you to transcend the experience gaps and the generational differences. For example, when you share your life history, focus on how you felt rather than on what happened. You could say, "I was nine the first time someone betrayed me. I felt so sad when my friend Jackie tattled on me and then didn't tell the truth" rather than "When I was nine, I told my friend Jackie that I had taken money from my mother's wallet. She told her sister, and her sister called my mom. When I confronted her, Jackie said she didn't tell. But I knew she had because . . ."

Can you spot the difference? Notice how the tone of the second conversation has changed. The narrative has taken on a familiarity, as if you are discussing a memory with a peer. Granted, the content of this message is not likely to be shared adult-to-adult, but the style of interaction is typical of a peer relationship. When you use this style of conversation with kids, they naturally assume an egalitarian relationship. Equals. Peers.

Peer relationships are reciprocal. I give and you give; over time intimacy is possible. We are in charge of how the relationship develops. A helping relationship is quite different. As a helper, I am in service to the child. I am a conduit for the child's exploration, learning, or perspective. I give without expectation, unconditionally. Helpers need friends and children need friends, but helpers can't ever be the peers of those they serve.

Being an adult in kids' lives demands that you meet kids where they are. In fact, they are developmentally incapable of meeting you. Kids can pretend to have skills beyond their years and they can act as if they are adults, but they really can't be your equal. Besides, they don't need another peer relationship. They need adults with whom they can identify; they need adults to emulate and respect. They need guides for the journey, not more friends on the same bus.

The best thing of all is that kids respond well to our most positive attributes. If you are willing to listen, laugh, applaud, remember, confide, trust, and cooperate, then you can make a difference in your work with children. With these interpersonal skills, you will easily fill the job description of a "Kid Advocate." (See "Adult Job Description" on page 8 for "Kid Advocate" qualifications.)

THE BASIC COMMUNICATION RULES

What qualifies you to be a guide for kids? Think about it. A guide gives good information and is understandable, and a guide has past experience. In other words, the two key dimensions necessary to take on this role are *effective communication* and *prior experience*. Age generally ensures experience; effective communication skills can be acquired.

You are not a communicator because you have language or intellect. Although both language and intellect help, skilled communicators are evaluated by their ability to listen well and to send messages clearly and succinctly. When you are working with kids, this can become a complicated process. Talking down to kids or assuming that you understand their feelings never works. Your best bet is clarity.

To be clear and to enhance the effectiveness of your communication, you can learn eight different communication rules, listed and explained on the following pages. The successful application of these rules requires diligence and patience.

1. Attend to the Speaker

Give nonverbal cues that you are listening, solicit continued input through verbal acknowledgment, and make contact so kids know you are "with" them. (If you are planning dinner, paying bills, or correcting papers while you listen, you are *not* attending.) Clear your mind. Sweep

Adult Job Description

Position: Kid advocate

Structure

Rules that make sense

Reasonable consequences

Relationships with caring and nurturing adults

Opportunities for work and play

Positive social outlets

Harmonious relationships

Critical-thinking practice

Safe environments

Informal support networks

Healthy expectations

Spontaneous play

Sensitive role models

Decision-making opportunities

Realistic perspective of the future (not fear-laden)

Offsetting blame and scapegoating

Fun experiences

Skills

Creative and reflective thinking

Effective communication

Industriousness in work and play

Proficient cooperation strategies

Empathy toward others

Competent planning processes and strategies

Valuing relationships

Positive use of personal talents

Flexibility

Belief in self

Perseverance when challenged

Problem-solving capability

Clear internal dialogue to help set boundaries

Positive use of humor

Support

Sense of self-worth

Personal sense of mastery

Assertiveness about asking for help

Development of informal support systems

Close, positive relationships

Healthy choices and needs

Appropriate risk taking

Chances for personal success

Interpersonal sensitivity

Problem-solving opportunities

Forecasting for the future

Willingness to delay gratification

Expressing and managing emotions

Developing a sense of humor

Learning from mistakes

out the debris. *Listen.* Now you have the opportunity to pay attention. Listening is the basis for all good communication. It stops *you* from talking. In fact, some of the best dialogues I have with kids require very few words from me.

2. Paraphrase the Speaker

"I hate school and all my teachers!"

"You hate school . . . You don't like your teachers."

Report in your own words what you heard from the sender of the message. Only paraphrase when you need to check information, to affirm agreements, or to verify a message. Don't run circles around the kids, parroting, "I hear you saying . . ." As soon as you try, you'll get retorts such as "Of course you do—I just said it!" or "Why are you talking like that?" Paraphrasing is a skill, not a style of interaction. Be cautious with its use. Sometimes, particularly when overused, a paraphrase sounds officious and staged.

3. Reflect the Speaker's Feelings

"I don't want to go home. I hate my dad."

"When you say that, I get a real sense of fear."

This skill is difficult to master but really simple once the basic premise is understood. Success here relies on your ability to paraphrase content and then go to the next step by adding a feeling statement based on your understanding of what has been said.

Let me demonstrate: If Sally says, "I don't want to go home— I hate my dad," a paraphrase would be, "You hate your dad." So far, so good. If you want to make this into a reflection-of-feeling statement, add a feeling statement based on *your* experience. For example: "When you talk about not wanting to go home and hating your dad, I get a *real sense of fear.*" My own experience is reflected. Why? Because I want to mirror for this young person not only *what* she said, but my *experience* of her message. Done well, this method leads to another level of dialogue: The mirroring technique may be the impetus for moving into a more intimate or cohesive relationship. It relies on your ability to congruently communicate the feelings.

You don't have to be correct in your affective assessment. After all, your reflection of the speaker's feelings is meant to be your opinion; consequently, you cannot be wrong.

Going back to the example of Sally, her retort might be "I am *not* afraid! I hate him because of what he does to my mom." Now you have another opening. Sally is setting the stage for additional dialogue. She is allowing you to engage comfortably and nonintrusively in an intimate conversation.

You have shared your experience. Sally is leading, and you have danced with her. You haven't told her how she feels. You don't claim to have shared her experience. You simply report what is obvious to you: "I got a real sense of fear as you were talking." This strategy takes the burden of explanation off the child and provides you, the listener, with a safe way to reflect emotional data.

In all my years working with kids, reflection of the speaker's feelings is the skill I employ the most. It keeps *me* out of the way; I don't consume the process with *my* thinking or advice. My message is clear and clean.

4. Summarize the Conversation

 "I can't do all my work. I have to go to my *job!*"

 "You don't have enough time between school and work . . ."

Collapsing the content of a dialogue into statements is most often used when you want to check agreements, contracts, or lists. Summarization provides the vehicle to make sure all parties are singing from the same songbook and on the same page. Some examples:

After a three-hour picnic-planning meeting,
the person who called the meeting summarizes:
"I will bring the paper plates, silver, and condiments. Mary is responsible for ordering the chicken and reserving the park. Bud will bring the drinks, and Hilda has agreed to take care of the salads. Mr. Carey will bring the kids on the bus."

After a 45-minute parent-teacher meeting, the teacher summarizes:

"So, Billy can only pass this class if he turns in the three late assignments, attends all classes between now and the end of the semester, is on time for all classes, and completes future assignments appropriately."

At the end of a one-hour family counseling session, the counselor summarizes:

"Let me check to make sure that we are all clear. Billy has agreed to work with a tutor three nights a week. During this time, his chores will be limited to keeping his room clean. Mrs. Smith will check Billy's homework every night and will stay in touch with his teacher. We will meet weekly."

Attending, paraphrasing, reflecting the speaker's feelings, and summarizing are primary communication skills. They ask the receiver of a message to "mirror" the content of the message being delivered. If every person working with kids followed these rules, we would dramatically improve our daily interactions with kids.

When you've mastered the first four rules, go on to the next four: *self-disclosure, interpreting behavior, probing sparingly,* and *giving feedback.* These higher order skills require more effort to learn and to use.

---

5. In Your Role as Helper, Use Self-Disclosure Only for the Benefit of the Recipient

"At times I have felt lonely, too . . ."

Wow! Someone knows how I feel!

Self-disclosure refers to talking about self, reporting personal experiences, sharing opinions, and offering personal perceptions. Generally, we tend to view our life experiences as the most valuable offering in a helping relationship. Nothing could be further from the truth!

With our adult friends, we engage in a repartee of sharing information and disclosing personal information. I say the name of the college I attended; you offer your alma mater as a point of perspective and a way to add to the conversation. In this reciprocal process, I talk and you talk, covering a myriad of topics—we dance together.

But this model is inappropriate in a helping relationship. *Helpers are not involved in a reciprocal process.* The helping process is solicitous. Our job is to help kids help themselves. No magic or mystery. Some of the best help comes when people are given an opportunity to talk about themselves.

In a helping relationship, self-disclosure should benefit the recipient. After a kid tells you he's lonely, you might say, "At times I have felt so lonely that I cried." Then leave it there; don't go into the details of your memory of loneliness. Don't overtalk. Punctuate the dialogue with your self-disclosing remarks, but don't overtake the conversation. The comments you make should be of benefit to the recipient. Check to make sure that your comments don't redirect attention from the student to you.

Self-disclosure is a vital aspect of interaction and communication. Only you can truly decipher those relationships that should be assigned to the "peer" realm and those in which you are a "helper." If the individual in front of you is a kid, that person is *not* a peer.

Here are some basic rules that work consistently if you do elect to disclose in a helping relationship.

Tell the truth.

Too often we protect kids by disguising the truth. While it is not necessary to share *all* your secrets or the full content of your experience, it is vital that you share your feelings accurately. That level of vulnerability is imperative in developing a relationship of influence.

Be quick and to the point.

Don't drag the disclosure out and weave multiple plots, innuendos, and possibilities. Give quick, nonjudgmental statements in the language of feeling, framed by "I": "I am feeling sad that this is going on for you. I wish I could make it go away, but I can't. I am so sorry."

Respect the recipient.

You are the *listener*. Make sure your comments in no way detract from the talker. Keep your roles straight.

Honor the differences.

You cannot fully understand another individual's pain or dilemma. Your experiences don't translate in a helping relationship. As peers, yes. In a helping relationship, no. Don't assume you understand. Put the burden back on the talker to explain and expose the meaning of what has been shared. Instead of "I understand," say, "Help me understand."

Let the kids do the work.

People who overtalk or inappropriately disclose in a helping relationship usually do so unconsciously. The conversation triggers something inside, and they lose control over the process. Slow down and remember you are the helper, the facilitator, the guide. The kid *needs* to do the work; the "work" is taking the responsibility to engage in a meaningful way with an adult, a helper. In a helping relationship, the helper solicits from the student without expecting a reciprocal repartee. The dialogue needs to be kid-centered; the kid's insight and awarenesses, not the helper's, should drive the conversation.

6. Interpret Behavior

Does his alarm work? Is he sleeping okay?

"I couldn't do my homework. I got up too late . . ."

Synthesize behavioral clues through personal filters. From this synthesis, judgments can be made or opinions formed. For every interpretive statement, behaviors have been filtered so quickly that no notice is taken of the process. Some people are so good at interpretation that they cannot pinpoint the behavioral clues to which they reacted. Sometimes we call this "intuition." For example, you might say, "Nancy, are you sick?" You interpreted a change in skin color (pallor), a lack of eye contact, and Nancy's refusal to join you for lunch, and you came up with illness as a likely explanation.

Be careful. The interpretive process and the judgments made as a result of it may get you into trouble if you use your conclusion as fact. Then you risk getting into conflicts: You have interpreted the information, and the recipient is compelled to refute the erroneous data.

Try this approach instead: "Nancy, when you walked into class today, I noticed that you seemed preoccupied. I thought you looked as though you had been crying. I assumed you were upset and opted not to ask you for your report today." This approach lets Nancy know two important pieces of information: what you saw and how you interpreted her behavior.

Using this method will typically open up a dialogue such as "I *was* crying. I saw a car hit a dog on my way to school, and it really threw me for a loop." Now you and Nancy are communicating.

The filter process is amazing. I have had innumerable experiences that have demonstrated the uniqueness of how we filter data. My best story occurred at a recent training.

When asked to draw a star, I drew:

Others drew:

The man sitting next to me drew:

 and said it was Rod Stewart.

Everybody lives in a different world.
We only share the planet.

7. Probe Sparingly

"I missed you today . . . I always wonder what happens during your day."

The probe is one of the most often-used techniques in communication, but its value is questionable. If I had my way, we would stop asking questions and commit to making statements. Let me explain.

The *probe* refers to direct questions, whether open-ended or closed. By not targeting a specific response, *open-ended questions* allow greater content to be shared. For example, the open-ended question "How has this chapter impacted your beliefs about communication?" requires an explanation as a response. *Closed questions* are usually asked for specific responses. For example, "Did you read the chapter about communication?" calls for only a yes or no answer. The communication comes to an abrupt halt.

Obviously, there is a need for both kinds of questions. As a quality communicator, you will need to format your questions to reflect the information required. Don't ask for more than you need and don't try to trick kids into talking. Kids pick up quickly on insincere gestures for soliciting conversation.

When it comes to kids, asking questions is like a death threat unless you have a prior history or relationship. Even in a classroom setting, kids will wait to see how and what you expect when asking questions. Too often adults ask but then answer on their own, either because their solicitation was phony or because the students were not given enough time to process the question. Either way, kids are cautious about questions, probably because they are constantly probed beyond what is reasonable. Think of how often parents do this:

"How was your day?"
"Were you late for school?"
"Did you get the lunch money from your dad?"
"How was soccer practice?"
"Did Billy get kicked off the team?"

The responses range from "Fine" and "Yeah" to "I dunno" and "No."

The rule is basic: *Ask questions only when you need specific information.* Make statements instead. This invites communication. For example, Mom could say: "I missed you today. I realize that our worlds are far apart. I wish I could be more a part of yours. I always wonder what happens during your day."

These more general statements—and the absence of questions—allow the kid to *choose* whether or not to engage in conversation with you. Giving kids a choice gives them control. Having a sense of control is vital in an adult-child relationship. So many other forces give the adult more control.

Do the kids a favor and let them choose whether or not they want to talk to you. If you are interesting, patient, and tenacious, the time will come when conversation occurs more easily. I promise. Your daughter may not be willing to go to the neighborhood mall with you, but she may talk with you in the car on the way to a mall out of town. Some of your students will have difficulty in an exchange with you when classmates are listening, but they may be more available after class or in a less threatening situation. Use the classroom as a home base for learning activities. The more varied the activities and strategies for dialogue, the more likely you are to tap into a style or scenario that will engage a majority of the students.

Engaging kids without questions lets them know that you value their input; trust that they have the skill to engage with you. Following this rule provides a classic model for emulation: You ask the kids to do as you have done. Refining the probe means giving up control and seeking nondemanding responses. Tough stuff, but worth the effort.

8. Give Constructive Feedback

"I'm really worried about how you're making decisions about school . . ."

Giving feedback often means confronting—not in an oppositional sense, but with care and concern. One of my colleagues calls this "carefrontation"; I like the term. Many people are afraid of confrontation, however well intended. "Confrontation" and "conflict" are among the nastiest words in the English language. Because of the bad rap confrontation has acquired over the years, I have opted to call this skill "giving constructive feedback."

A coach trying to encourage a football player to keep his head up and his eye on the action may use constructive feedback: "Hey, Billy, I liked what you did out there. Nice job. Try to keep your head up after the catch—makes it easier in the long run."

Constructive feedback, used by those in the role to assess performance (teachers, coaches, parents), provides important information about personal behaviors and attitudes as measured against conventional norms. For our purposes, this kind of feedback is given when our students are judged to be in harm's way or without the resources to assess themselves realistically.

Feedback is also given in situations where positive gains have occurred, but communicating the positive is usually not difficult. Rather, the negative or problematic data too often go unsaid. The unsaid, unreported, unconfronted data usually fester and create long-term negative consequences. A general rule of thumb is that it is best to be in the moment with any concern—positive or negative.

Don't give feedback in unsolicited circumstances—unless your role or relationship has an inherent feedback clause. A teacher, for example, doesn't have to wait for students to inquire about their performance. A teacher's job requires giving feedback to students as an essential aspect of completing assigned tasks.

In areas where feedback is not required, why would you want to go to the trouble? Because it can make a difference! As the basis for intervention, constructive feedback starts a change process. It can also help keep relationships from being burdened by secrets—by truths untold. For example, rarely do family members confront someone who is alcoholic. More likely, they try to live as long as possible as if nothing is wrong. This same phenomenon occurs within the classroom. Cheating goes on without consequences because the students don't want to get involved. Or a student with family problems drops out of school because she perceives the burden of her secrets to be too great.

Kids often get caught in secret traps, and they sometimes try to trap helpers: "I'll tell you, but you can't tell . . ." "If I tell, you must . . ." For many young people, sharing secrets is the evidence of intimacy. Solicitation for secrecy is often a call for greater closeness. However, helpers must be cautious of these potential traps. If warnings are unheeded, helpers may end up held hostage by information they have agreed not to share.

I know a second year teacher who promised strict confidentiality for student journals. One student articulated a desire to commit suicide. The teacher did nothing and the student died after his first suicide attempt. The parents found the journal after his death and brought suit against the teacher. While this is an extreme case, the teacher should have immediately confronted the student.

Feedback is a vital skill in any helping relationship, allowing us—as parents, teachers, counselors, helpers of kids—to be the best we can be. Without feedback, kids have only their own eyes and their own filters. That can be too limiting and too narrow a vision.

Here are some rules to help you give constructive feedback.

Restrict your comments to behaviors and situations that can be changed.

Be specific. Report verifiable data. If you don't know, say so.

Come from a caring—not a scaring—place.

Report your feelings. Feedback is meant to help, not destroy. When feedback has a negative agenda, it becomes a weapon.

Give options to help manage the needed change.

Discuss resources; offer to be a part of the next step.

Prepare your comments in advance.

Debrief any negative emotions and be prepared to control your feelings.

Know that feedback is a gift.

Wrap it well. Find a safe place to deliver it. Make preparations to be heard.

Pay attention to your tone.

Use an even tone so you don't add additional data to the messages being sent. The wrong tone may obscure the content.

Grab your pants or skirt.

What? Gestures will also add information to the presentation and feedback session. Keep your hands to your sides or hold onto something if necessary. Too often gestures add information that is incongruent with the verbalized message.

For example, I recently worked with a second grade teacher who couldn't understand why her kids seemed to be afraid of her. After a brief observation of her in front of her students, I clearly saw the source of her problem: She karate-chopped her left hand with her right whenever she was trying to make a point. The kids' heads went up and down with her hand gestures. Rather than hearing what she said, they interpreted the gestures as some kind of threat. Her hand signals overwhelmed her verbal message.

Prepare to manage the reactions.

Don't get "woofed," distracted, or diverted from the point of the conversation. Classic "woofs" are belligerence, cursing, crying, walking away, or even projecting blame. Kids are good at these manipulations. What do you know about this person? How has this person reacted in similar situations? Can you handle the response? If not, get help. If you need a facilitator, the feedback strategy becomes "intervention."

The best feedback usually involves three kinds of information: *behavioral, emotional,* and *consequential.* I like to borrow from Vern Johnson (the creator of interventions for alcoholics and the founder of the Johnson Institute) and use "I saw," "I felt," and "I did (or will do)."[2] The actual conversation is brief and should take no more than three minutes. You should be fully in charge. Don't take on the pain, shame, or blame. A confrontation might sound something like this:

> ***Teacher to student:***
> "Billy, I got really confused reading your assignment last night. It was poorly written and barely legible. You answered only two of the five questions and misread one of the questions that you did answer. I wouldn't be so concerned about this one assignment if I hadn't also noticed an increase in tardies for my class. And, frankly, I miss talking with you—we don't seem to talk anymore. I wish I knew what to do. I do know that this work is not satisfactory. I am willing to give you until Friday to figure out how to make up this assignment. If you choose not to make it up, the failing grade will stand. Let me know if I can help."

Notice that there is very little opportunity for response. The goal of the confrontation is not necessarily to create a dialogue. Needed information is provided safely and succinctly. Guesses and maybes are eliminated.

Speak slowly and deliberately, and stay focused on the point; don't get woofed. Some situations require patience just to be heard:

Mom to daughter:
"Katy, I overheard that you are planning to go to the beach after fifth period with Becky . . ." "No, I wasn't listening in on the phone; besides, that's not the point. I'm really worried about how you're making decisions about school lately . . ." "Just let me talk for a minute. This is the third incident of ditching a class in the last three weeks. I can't help but notice that it is always with Becky. I don't know what is going on. I'm scared—and worried. I have always told you that my job in your life is to keep you safe. Something is wrong here, and I am unwilling to just let it go . . ." "No, I won't stop worrying if you agree to go to school tomorrow. This is bigger than one day at the beach. I think we need help. I want to find us a counselor . . ."

Remember, you are not in charge of the receiver's reactions. You are not responsible for the response your confrontation elicits. Feedback is a gift, given unconditionally. If the message you share is coming from a caring place, you won't need to plan how the other person will respond.

Giving constructive feedback is the riskiest of all communication, going beyond honesty and vulnerability to a *sacred* place—caring so much that you are willing to risk losing the relationship. The level of risk varies with the nature of the relationship. But do not try to compare levels of risk; do not judge any risk as greater than another. All helping relationships have the potential to effect a shift in the child's quality of life, and all relationships need to be valued.

The eight rules of communication given here are meant as guidelines for adult-child relationships. There will always be exceptions and circumstances warranting different responses. Don't get caught in the trap of viewing these guidelines as mandates; they are merely suggestions. Don't expect perfection; try to increase your skill over time.

The best barometer of successful communication is the receiver of your message. Check it out: Are you being heard as you intended?

THE SOURCES OF INFORMATION

Learning how to establish an effective dialogue with kids is aided when various sources of information are used in the context of the conversation. It is important to identify the sources of concern, the sources of input, and the sources motivating the interaction.

To be clear, use all eight communication skills in conjunction with the three domains from which information can be gleaned: *knowing, perceiving,* and *feeling.* Each domain adds another level of information to the messages sent.

Knowing

To know is to have factual information, verifiable data, or data accepted without question. What do I know? What is factual and what is hearsay? What is truth and what is opinion?

Facts:
Billy hasn't turned in any homework assignments for two weeks. He has been late for class two times this week, and he has fallen asleep in class four times over the past two weeks.

Facts:
My daughter Katy Jeanne was born in Santa Rosa on March 2, 1988. She weighed 6 pounds, 12 ounces.

These are facts. In communicating we often elaborate upon the facts, coming up with impressions of the truth.

Impression:
Billy has been going out with his friends every night instead of doing his homework and getting a good night's sleep.

Impression:
Katy Jeanne was a pretty baby—the cutest baby in the whole nursery.

Operating as if our truth is everyone's reality is faulty communication. Making these quasi-facts into nonrefutable statements gets us into trouble because our "facts" become fodder for criticism and refutation. "Katy was the prettiest baby in the nursery to me." Now this is a personal statement of fact reflecting my opinion. Once I own the statement, I become the verifier, the fact maker.

Perceiving

To perceive is to guess, to have beliefs or opinions, to interpret, or to judge. Talking about my perceptions—my guesses, opinions, and interpretations—is far easier than talking about facts. I do this all the time with my peers, who view my remarks as being biases with a personal focus.

When dealing with kids, let them know how you perceive their thoughts and actions and why you came to the conclusion being expressed. Be clear. Often kids lack the savvy to discern the fine line between fact and opinion.

Kids are caught in a developmental dilemma. Everything said by an adult smells like a fact. This can create a potent and often painful reality for many kids. Mom says in anger, "He left because of you." The kid thinks, "It must be the truth—Mom said it was so. What is so bad about me that I made my dad leave? I must be bad, very bad." Mom has burdened her kid with an opinion voiced in anger when she was out of control. The kid doesn't comprehend this as a communication faux pas shared under stress.

The same situation happens in the classroom: "What's wrong with you?" "What do you mean, you don't understand?" "You lost our chance." Words that echo long after they are said. Words that haunt and hurt. If the words they use are said in the moment, said without thinking, adults can cause great pain.

Moms, dads, teachers, coaches, and all other adults, please take this to heart: Be careful what you say.

> ***Another story:***
> A man and three kids got on a bus. The kids were screaming and yelling. The man looked harried and overwhelmed. Two women were seated near the man and his children. One woman moved to the front of the bus in a huff and muttered, "He should be able to control his children." The second woman smiled and asked if she could help. A tear fell down the man's cheek. He said, "I'm sorry. My wife just died. The kids really . . ." He didn't have to say any more. She understood.

The man's comment helped the second woman *accurately* perceive the situation. From this new perspective, she could take appropriate action. A paradigm shift.

Feeling

Feelings are *your* label of *your* experiences in emotional terms.

Until early adolescence, most kids know three feeling states: *sad, mad,* and *glad.* Not only do they have limited experience, they assume that their feelings at the moment are their experience. Many younger children (ages five to ten) will say things like "I am the happiest I have ever been" or "I hate Billy—I will never speak to him again" or "I'll never have another friend like Karen—I am so sad she moved away." The feelings are black and white. Sad is sad. Mad is mad. Glad is great.

Then comes adolescence. Hit by the hormone train, adolescents are beset by feelings that are difficult to sort out and understand. Much of the time, they'll use language that is contradictory: "I think I am so hurt . . ." "I hate loving him . . ." "I dunno . . ." "I don't care." Their language and their experience are confused, incongruent, and out of control. To bridge the developmental schism, young people need to learn the language of feelings. They must also have permission to express their feelings without fear of put-downs or having their feelings discounted.

All feelings must be validated; all feelings are real.

No exceptions. Adults can make a difference just by listening—not fixing, not advising. Approach kids with a willingness to respect their feelings and I can guarantee a relationship. When you let kids know you understand their feelings, you've become a helper.

Most feelings have roots in the three basic feeling states of sad, mad, and glad. This is rather like all colors coming from the three primary colors of red, yellow, and blue. I have fun exploring the breadth and depth of kids' feelings.

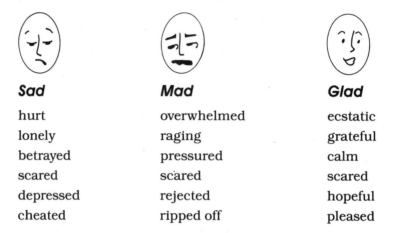

Sad	*Mad*	*Glad*
hurt	overwhelmed	ecstatic
lonely	raging	grateful
betrayed	pressured	calm
scared	scared	scared
depressed	rejected	hopeful
cheated	ripped off	pleased

This list was compiled by a fifteen-year-old girl in answer to the question "What have you felt during this last week?" Clearly, the author of this list has had varied experiences. Her feeling labels approximate her experiences. She uses these labels to describe feelings that are familiar. She uses the same term in different situations. She even has the same feelings with different origins, and if confronted she might very well deny a feeling altogether.

What makes up her very complicated feeling repertoire is not duplicated anywhere in the universe. Her feelings are a part of her experience, memories, hopes, and dreams. They are uniquely hers and need to be valued as the treasures that they are. Please: *Value feelings; don't try to make sense of them.*

COMMUNICATION SKILLS IN FIVE DIALOGUES

Communication skills and the three sources of information—knowing, perceiving, and feeling—are fascinating study areas. Unfortunately, having this information does not ensure "doing it right" in the moment of import. Let's look at some sample dialogues addressing three issues with kids often discussed by parents and teachers:

1. setting rules

2. motivating efforts toward school

3. managing negative choices

I have tried to narrate realistic responses to real-life situations.

Setting Rules

Scenario:

Tanya is eleven. She is popular and is becoming very social. Suddenly, family is second to friends. She is preoccupied and hasn't completed a chore without a hassle in two months. Mom and Dad are at their limit. Tanya blithely moves along. This is a family meeting. Tanya only knows that the phone is off the hook. She suspects she is in trouble. Her best friend, Tamra, says that family meetings are tricks parents use to get you to do things.

Scene:

The Williams family is in the kitchen. Two coffee cups are on the table.

Tanya: So what did I do now?

Mom: Tanya, this isn't about what you've done. It *is* about how we are living together as a family.

Tanya: Yeah. So, like what else do I have to do?

Dad: Tanya, your chores are important. But this meeting is about how we are acting and being a family.

Tanya: Huh?

Mom: Let's figure out what all of us are thinking about our family. What are the benefits of being a Williams?

Dad: I like knowing that you guys will be there when I get home. I am not ever lonely. I like having a partner to do things with. I like to think that I teach Tanya good stuff. I don't think about this kind of thing very often.

Mom: I like being a Williams because I want to belong somewhere. I don't feel left out. I want to be important to people. I like sharing money responsibility. And I like going to sleep feeling safe.

Tanya: I know it's my turn—I hate this, Mom. I like to be a Williams 'cause kids think Dad is cool. He makes me good cakes and he tells good jokes and he wrestles with me and he tells you not to hassle me too much.

Mom: So we all have different reasons. I forgot a *big* reason: I love you guys.

Tanya: I love you, too.

Dad: That's a fact!

Mom: How do you show your love for us, Robert?

Dad: I do things with you. I go to work and share expenses. I would protect you if I thought you were in danger. I think about you when you are not with me.

Tanya: I *hate* this. How long is this gonna take?

Mom: Not too much more time, Tanya. I think we are at an important point. Being part of this family requires that we all pull our share of the load. We want you to think about what is reasonable for you to do as part of your contribution. We are all getting different things from being a part of this family. Regardless of how we perceive what we get, we *all* have to be a part of how the family operates.

Dad: We have decided that we need three things from you: One, no more than one hour on the phone *after* homework. Two, one night on the weekends should be considered family night, and we'll negotiate which night. And three, before you go to anyone's house, we will call their parents.

Tanya: Daaaad! You're gonna make me into a nerd!

Mom: Tanya, there is one more thing. We want you to pick three chores that you'll be responsible for every week. Also, you need to figure out what should happen to you if you don't follow through on your chores. Your allowance will be based on getting all three chores done. I would like it if you would help me put together another list of chores that you might do and how much they are worth to you. Then you can make extra money if you need it. You are in charge, Tanya. We don't want to spend the next few years yelling about beds not being made. Help us out here . . .

Dad: Your mom and I also figure that we should meet like this once a month. We don't want to miss talking to you or get too busy and stop talking altogether. You are a *big deal* in our lives. We love you.

Mom: You got that right!

Tanya: Mom, stop it. Can I call Tamra now?

Dad: Well, I'm glad that's over . . .

This script is intended as a guide, not a verbatim outline. Preparation of a script when you are challenged to deal with big issues can be a big help. I have repeatedly found that the greater the level of preparation, the greater the success of the interaction.

What had to happen before this dialogue could take place?

1. Mom and Dad had to get organized.

2. Some agreements had to be negotiated prior to the discussion. This ensured that the significant contributors were on the same page of the script (at the same time).

3. Mom and Dad practiced.

4. A sequence of events was determined.

5. Selection of crucial outcomes was delineated.

These five steps describe a classic intervention strategy that can be applied in numerous settings with varied audiences. A major thrust for the parents in this dialogue was to refrain from contradicting each other or from making anyone in the family the bad guy. Tanya was clearly trying to get Mom's attention when she articulated benefits in the family only in relation to her father. Since Tanya's mother did not take Tanya's comments personally, the focus remained on family life and responsibility.

Some of you reading this might think, "What about spontaneity and going with the flow?" Spontaneity and flexibility are potent relationship characteristics. Without them, relationships do not survive change. I am not talking about planning and scripting interactions of intimacy. I am not even talking about everyday interactions. Rather, in times of crisis or uncertainty, you need to think carefully before you speak.

Too often things are said in pain and anger that are never erased from memory when the crisis is over. Plan what you say. Take the responsibility to control the messages you send regardless of what is going on. Practice helps.

My ten commandments for adults in kids' lives

1. Praise well and often.

2. Give kids opportunities to control and to choose.

3. Look for the positive in all situations.

4. Be responsible and give responsibility.

5. Validate feelings.

6. Focus on what it will take to make it right, to make it better, or to make it different.

7. Help each other be right.

8. Be what you want kids to be.

9. Play more, laugh more, and do more with them.

10. Create memories that will serve the kids for a lifetime.

Motivating Efforts Toward School

The next three scripts employ these ten commandments.

Scenario:
Anton, age eight, hates school. He doesn't want to go, and he thinks his teacher doesn't like him.

Scene:
Mom and Anton are in the car on the way to a doctor's appointment.

Anton: Thanks for letting me go to the doctor's during school, Mom.

Mom: What?

Anton: I like getting outta school.

Mom: I used to like getting out of school, too, Anton.

Anton: Did you hate school, Mom?

Mom: No, but sometimes the work got so hard that I felt like everybody understood but me.

Anton: I know. Like, I don't even get division, and now they're doing fractions! I don't get it at all.

Mom: Well, I understand fractions. Can I give you an example?

Anton: Yeah.

Mom: Remember when we went to Chuck E. Cheese for your birthday?

Anton: I like Chuck E. Cheese!

Mom: When you told me you wanted to invite eight friends to the party, I had to figure out how many pizzas to order. You said each kid could eat three pieces of pizza. Each pizza had twelve pieces, and we needed twenty-four pieces. So how many pizzas did we get?

Anton: Two!

Mom: Right, Anton. We got two pizzas because three pieces was one-fourth of a whole pizza, so eight kids would eat two pizzas. That's working with fractions.

Anton: Mom, school never makes it that easy. The teacher likes to talk about stuff I don't under-stand at all.

Mom: Want to make a bet?

Anton: I guess so.

Mom:	Okay. I bet you and I can figure out this school stuff. How about if we meet just after dinner on Tuesdays and Thursdays?
Anton:	What if it doesn't work?
Mom:	Anton, we've got to find a way to make school work for you. School is really important for your future. Learning things like fractions makes being a grown-up much easier. Let's stop for tacos on our way home. Maybe we can figure out another example of fractions—like I'll pay only nine-tenths of the bill and you'll pay one-tenth!

Motivation for Anton was framed by an initial success, a challenge, and the willingness of the parent to "do" with the child.

Here's another dialogue that shows how to motivate efforts toward school.

Scenario:

Tim, age thirteen, hates math. He has never succeeded at math, and his math teacher, Mrs. Jones, is convinced that his negative attitude is sabotaging his learning.

Scene:

Mrs. Jones has asked Tim to stay after class for a few minutes so they can talk privately.

Mrs. Jones:	Did you have trouble finding today's class assignment?
Tim:	I can't do it, and I don't care what you say.
Mrs. Jones:	That is a really powerful statement. You must really believe that this is impossible.
Tim:	Yeah, so I . . .
Mrs. Jones:	Let's start over, Tim. Make the slate clean. Pretend this is your first day in my class.
Tim:	This is weird . . .
Mrs. Jones:	I know. Other kids have called me that, too. Play along with me?
Tim:	Yeah.
Mrs. Jones:	My name is Mrs. Jones. I am your math teacher this semester. I teach math because I used to hate it, but my father helped me see that math is needed for everything to work in the world. I like math—now. What is your favorite subject?

Tim:	I really like sports and stuff.
Mrs. Jones:	Help me understand why you like sports.
Tim:	Well—you get to run and yell, and everybody thinks it's cool when you do something for the team. The coach is really cool, and he likes to tell you that you're good and how to get better. Oh, and another thing—other kids can help you get stuff done.
Mrs. Jones:	Okay. I think I understand. Sports is a good thing because you believe that you can be successful, that others can help, and that your coach believes in your abilities.
Tim:	I don't think I said all that . . .
Mrs. Jones:	You gave me some great ideas for our class. We'll get this math thing done together.

One of the best ideas to try is helping the student reframe the situation from negative to positive. In this dialogue, Mrs. Jones was able to end the conversation positively by reframing the concern, offering alternatives, and creating a hook for follow-up (that Tim is not alone).

Managing Negative Choices

Scenario:
Teresa, age twelve, is very popular and likes the attention she gets. She hurt a friend's feelings by snubbing her on the way to school.

Scene:
The counselor is talking with Teresa during lunch break. The counselor begins by talking in general.

Counselor:	So it was a good day? Great. I thought about you and hoped you were having fun with your new classes. Is Ann with you?
Teresa:	Ann is in three of my classes, but . . . the other kids don't like Ann, so I didn't eat lunch with her today. I don't see why I have to be with her . . . We don't see each other that much any more . . . I mean I still like her, but I really like my new friends . . .
Counselor:	Let me see if I've got this right: Ann is in three of your classes, but you opted not to sit with her at lunch because of your new friends.

Teresa: When you say it like that it sounds—like— really bad.

Counselor: Something does seem off. It doesn't seem very kind to snub Ann because of your new friends. I really don't understand . . . [The bell rings.] We can talk again tomorrow. Think about the situation. Sometimes it is helpful to imagine yourself in someone else's shoes . . .

Notice that everything does not have to be resolved in one conversation. Insight is often best realized when time allows the thought process to work. When things are left unresolved, be sure to provide a way to reconnect with the child.

Here's a more drastic way to manage negative choices.

Scenario:

Karen is seventeen. She lives with her father because since her parents' divorce she couldn't get along with her mother. She went out and got drunk, then drove the car home. Dad met her at the door at 2 A.M., two hours past her curfew, but decided not to confront her while she was drunk.

Scene:

The next morning at the kitchen table.

Dad: Karen, I spent most of the night thinking about you. I have some things I need to say, so I'm going to ask you to hold your comments. I have rehearsed this so I don't mess up. I think this is one of the most important things I have ever had to do as your dad.

Karen, loving you has been one of the greatest aspects of my life. I have a lot of memories that I can easily picture in my mind: your first step, going to school for the first time, learning to read. Throughout our life together, I have viewed my job as being your safety net. I kept you from running into the street. I taught you not to run with a sharp object in your hand, to duck when the ball was thrown too hard. We have talked about boys, about dating and sex. I am here to keep you safe.

Last night you violated three major rules: You came home two hours late, you were drinking, and you drove while you were drunk . . . No, it would not have been okay if you had gotten home on time, or if you had gotten drunk but then hadn't driven.

For some reason that I don't understand, alcohol is dangerous for us. I have had problems with it and so has your mother. Seeing you intoxicated scared the hell out of me. This is serious, so serious that I called a therapist today and set up an appointment for us at 11 o'clock . . . No, I am not going to work today. You are the most important work I've got to do.

When you came home drunk last night, I realized that all our talking and lecturing about alcohol hasn't made sense to you. You weren't born yet when your mother's drinking was bad, and I stopped after your third birthday. We have a big problem with booze in this family, and I want to keep you safe from the pain it can cause. I care about you; I love you—and I have to do what I think is right.

Because you failed to call and because you were home two hours late, I'm grounding you for one week. Because you drove drunk, I have enrolled you in a special driver's program that is held on Tuesday nights for six weeks. These are punishments. Because you got drunk, we have the appointment with the counselor. The counselor is not a punishment.

I hope you are willing to give the counseling process a chance. This is really important for all of us. I called your mom, and she'll meet us at the counselor's office. We both love you and we both care about what happens to you.

I know I haven't given you much input in this process. I am doing what I feel is the only right thing to do, and I need you to come along with me. When you were three, I didn't ask if you wanted me to pull you out from in front of a truck—I did it to keep you safe. That's what this is about: loving you and keeping you safe.

In this dialogue, *knowing* in advance what the consequences are is vital. Should Karen opt not to go to counseling, a second plan should be articulated. A rule to follow when confronting: Plan the getting out *before* you get in! Other hints follow.

GUIDELINES TO ENGAGE YOUNG PEOPLE

If you want to make connections and communicate well with kids in an influential way, if you truly want to make a difference, these reminders should help.

Get kids' attention!

Make sense, be clear, tell the truth, and be vulnerable.

Check your motivation.

Reaching out to a kid has got to be an unconditional process. There's no room for *your* stuff. Stay focused on the kid; take your needs elsewhere.

Know that talk is good.

Never underestimate the value and power of conversation. Engage kids in conversation, and you have the foundation for a positive relationship. Talk, talk, talk. And remember:

Talk about things that interest the kids.

Use self-disclosure only to solicit dialogue and validate feelings.

Do not talk to kids as if they are your peers.

Talking while doing is better than just talking.

Dialogue improves when you do things together. When the doing is fun, the relationship becomes special.

Use the language of feelings.

Your feelings, described in a simple manner, help kids learn to express themselves. Your willingness to expose emotion provides an opportunity to connect. Feelings and laughter are great conduits for intimacy.

Understand that everyone views life uniquely.

We all have different filters framed by our own experiences. No two people are alike. No two people respond the same way to the same situation. Respect the different filters; find out how people *see* before you judge.

Don't speak in anger—report anger.

"I was angry . . ." That is a statement of feelings. Separate feeling states from content and causes. Otherwise damaging messages like "I wish you had never been born" and "I hate you" are said in anger and create potential lifelong consequences. Speaking *in* anger is not a good choice. Reporting anger will communicate your concerns without the potentially damaging out-of-control statement.

Plan the getting out before you get in.

Plan and practice. If you have something important to say to someone, plan your scenario and practice your script. Try it out on a mirror, a friend, a psychotherapist. Practice will help.

Be time smart.

Don't try to do everything at once. Painting dreams takes time and planning, testing and distancing, and a little dancing between partners. Making memories is an incredible job—the potential is there at every turn and in every interaction. You have the power and the opportunity to make memories. Make them good ones.

THE USE OF ONE-LINERS

Sometimes you won't have the time or the opportunity to create the repartee necessary to make a teaching point, but you will still want to get your message across quickly and positively. The following one-liners can provide the segue that helps create the opportunity for more interaction. A conversation can be redirected in less than a moment. Sarcasm is out; vulnerability and humor are in. Here are some ideas to try in response to kids' negativity.

> ***I hate it.***
> I need help to understand why.
> Or: I only hate liver.
> Or: How does "hate" feel for you?

> ***I can't do it.***
> Let's focus on what you *can* do.
> Or: What would [a sports figure or other famous person] say to someone who gave up?
> Or: Tell me what you want me to say.

> ***This is stupid.***
> I believe you think this is stupid.
> Or: Define "stupid."
> Or: I need to know what you mean.

> ***It's your fault.***
> What could I have done to ensure that this didn't happen?
> Or: I wish it had worked out differently.
> Or: I want to make this up to you.

Notice in all of these one-liners, the focus is positive. The helper assumes the position of vulnerability. Try to deflect blame, interrupt scapegoating, and never shame the kids. High expectations can help; don't lower your standards when kids are negative or when their behavior is out of the norm. Children need to be safe, and you can provide a sense of control by not reacting to negatives with negatives. Become a model for turning the negative into something positive.

THE IMPORTANCE OF COMMUNICATION

Every time I finish a lecture or workshop on the nature and skills of communication, someone invariably calls out that there's not enough time for all this. Then someone else adds that if teachers talk—that is, *really communicate*—with every kid who needs special attention, they would never be able to teach. They couldn't possibly get their work done. My retort is always the same: Make this a part of your work.

Educators need to move from teaching subject matter to working with kids. Teachers need to let go of "I teach math" and realize that they are no longer "telling" kids; they are "guiding" them. This reframing of a teacher's job description also requires a real shift in skill. Connecting with kids is our greatest challenge. Without these connections, we risk losing a generation. Connecting and communicating with kids, particularly those needing special attention, are essential skills for anyone serving in a helping capacity.

NOTES

1. H. Stephen Glenn and Jane Nelsen, *Raising Self-Reliant Children in a Self-Indulgent World* (Rocklin, CA: Prima, 1989).

2. Vern Johnson, *I'll Quit Tomorrow* (New York: HarperCollins, 1980).

CHAPTER 2

Communicating with Kids in Group Settings

LEARNING TO WORK WITH KIDS in groups will enhance your skills repertoire. Groups broaden the scope of helping and provide an arena to better understand self. Most kids find group experiences personally beneficial, fun, and insight provoking. Besides, groups are the natural way kids organize themselves. Learning to be an effective member of a group contributes to overall quality of life.

Time is short. We cannot help all those who need help or work on communicating effectively with all the kids who may be eager to listen. One of the most effective and time-efficient ways to help kids is to work with groups of kids who have mutual concerns.

It is not happenstance that many of the benefits of groups parallel the gains experienced by positive family units, teams, and staffs. Group process is one of the most effective tools to use while working with kids because kids help to reinforce group norms and establish a kind of peer check system that helps protect the group process. Because groups are such a powerful tool, I want to share some helpful hints about starting and running groups.

Groups form for a variety of reasons and begin at different task levels. For example, some groups start with clear tasks or outcomes, and members must learn to build cohesion and trust one another. A group started with clear tasks might be a study group organized to create the best possible learning environment for a given topic. I was part of a study group in grad school. The task was clear: survival in the business finance course. The group organized around the task and became social as time passed. When we finished the course, the group disbanded.

Other groups may come together with a shared purpose, and members must learn to become productive during the course of their experience with one another. A group with a shared purpose might be organized for a specific cause, like helping homeless people. As it evolves, the group defines its task.

As a group leader, you need to identify and align with positive forces. Form groups around "real" issues. These issues might include some shared pain (for example, addiction, death, suicide, loss, grief, anger, divorce, abandonment) or situations viewed negatively by a conventional majority (for example, drug abuse, precocious sex, HIV-AIDS, satanism, self-inflicted wounds). Issues with personal meaning draw people to group activities, but the "group chemistry" sustains members' involvement over the long haul.

Groups that have effective leadership and trained participants work best. Because the peer culture has such great influence, a group can become either a positive or a negative force. Certainly in this age of gangs and violence, we have seen that a group's culture can become antisocial. On the other hand, we have evidence of its equally potent positive influence, as seen when groups organize food drives, help people with disabilities, and reach out to those in need. Use the potency of the peer culture to your advantage by becoming an effective group leader.

THE DEVELOPMENTAL STAGES OF GROUPS

Group interaction is a process that generally improves over time. Most groups go through a series of developmental stages largely related to group cohesion or group chemistry, trust, productivity, and mission.

The chart on the next page presents Charles "Buzz" Blick's expansion of a model of group process originally proposed by Bruce W. Tuckman and Mary Ann C. Jensen.[1] This model replaces the linear concept of developmental stages with a more flexible description of team developmental needs. In every stage group members exhibit essential needs that must be met if they are to progress to the next level—that is, cope effectively with the challenges of the next level. Team "needs" reemerge as time passes, as membership changes, and as the goals of the team change. Recognition of the ongoing quality of team needs helps to explain why long-term group members sometimes appear to be working on issues (such as support, acceptance, and trust) that presumably were resolved during the early stages of team development.

Tuckman and Jensen characterize the forming stage as a time when members have a strong need to formulate goals and become personally committed to those goals. This initial period helps satisfy personal or "I" needs.

Once members understand and become personally committed to the team's goals, needs related to membership emerge. Tuckman and Jensen define this norming stage as a time when the group process, or the "we," becomes dominant. Members must confront issues of cooperation/competition, trust, leadership, and group decision making.

As team members successfully meet the challenges posed by the group—that is, work together productively while allowing for their individual differences—members' energy can be directed toward what Tuckman and Jensen call performance or "task" needs. The pressures members feel at this point are primarily directed toward the need to get their work done effectively and efficiently.

The Progression of Needs During Team Development

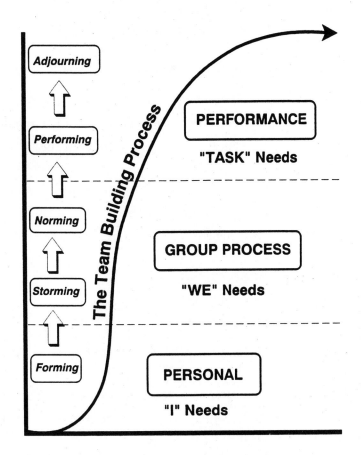

Note: Unpublished material. Copyright 1992 by Charles Blick. Reprinted by permission.

A group leader who knows both the stages of group development and the needs of the group members as they experience those stages can more easily move the group past common barriers. These predictable barriers, arising at different points in the stages of group development, are generally related more to specific process issues than to the content of the group work. Expect such challenges to surface and view them as opportunities to move a group from one stage to another.

The following guidelines can help group leaders move their members from one stage to the next:[2]

Steps to move group members from "I" to "We" stage

Utilize an objective facilitator

Develop a set of group agreements

Utilize a structured process to build safety and trust

Begin with a vision

Identify and align with positive forces; seize on hot issues

Identify and respect the individual values of the members; build these values into the activities of the group

Steps to move group members from "We" to "Task" stage

Develop a shared mission

Create positive goals for positive outcomes

Match the group's tasks with the level of group development

Structure specific short-term tasks

Design tasks for early success and easy gains

Copy the success of others; make it your own

Steps to sustain high performance

Utilize task-driven agendas

Structure for follow-up

Take time to celebrate the process, not just the successes

Learn from your process; evaluate and train

Recognize and celebrate the relationships among group members

Sustain long-term commitment

Effective Meeting Skills, by Marion Haynes, is one of the most useful guides to running group meetings. As Haynes so clearly states, "To be an effective leader you must be able to analyze each situation, determine what is needed to move forward, and take the necessary action to achieve the objectives."[3] The guidelines on the next page ("Adult Job Description" for meeting facilitator qualifications) are based generally on Haynes' work.

THE THREE TYPES OF GROUPS

All groups have the same dynamics, but groups of kids come together for three different reasons, making three discrete types of groups: *instructional groups*, *personal awareness groups*, and *skill-building groups*. Each type of group requires a different strategy on the part of the group leader. Also, each type of group has a discrete purpose within the context of helping kids. The following discussion should serve those interested in facilitating groups more effectively.

Adult Job Description

Position: Meeting facilitator

The leader's role is to monitor the activity in each key component area and provide the missing elements required to move the group toward the meeting's objectives.

Content

Initiate action

Keep on topic

Elicit information

Compare/contrast viewpoints

Summarize

Test for decisions

Develop action plans

Interaction

Monitor participation

Encourage participation

Model supportive behavior

Encourage building/supporting

Encourage differing/confronting

Facilitate conflict resolution

Explore reactions and feelings

Facilitate feedback among members

Structure

Develop agenda

State objectives

Manage time

Utilize procedures and techniques for:

    —recording/displaying data

    —analyzing data

    —generating alternatives

    —making decisions

    —making role assignments

    —developing ground rules

Note: From *Effective Meeting Skills: Practical Guide for More Productive Meetings* (p. 31), by Marion Haynes, 1988, Menlo Park, CA: Crisp Publications. Copyright 1988 by Crisp Publications. Adapted by permission.

Instructional Groups

Instructional groups are organized to impart information and increase knowledge. Leaders of instructional groups needn't shift curricula to utilize this type of group. Rather, a shift in emphasis is needed. The didactic material becomes useful and interesting when the students are challenged to be productive. Group process provides a way to achieve this end.

Members of an instructional group must have a clear sense of what the subject is and why group members need to learn about this subject. This is done most effectively when some kind of an introduction—a discussion of goals and expectations—precedes the actual instruction.

I have constructed guidelines for this strategy. The steps outlined here provide concrete ways to enhance the instructional group, and each step in the process is vital.

Step 1: Debrief the need for information

The best debriefings allow students to look at their need for information from a variety of perspectives. The aim is to figure out to whom the information is important, unimportant, and immaterial. This process can be a big deal for kids. As soon as you open the possibility that what is being taught has real value and connection to their quality of life, you have potentially opened minds.

The debriefing process can be described as having a life of its own. I often use the metaphor of dancing, with each step leading to another. The better we are at the dance, the more the information itself and how we access it become integrated. Helping debrief the need for and utility of information becomes a vital "sorting" process. The "sort" is a fancy description of how information is organized, valued, and perceived.

The debriefing stage sets up an interesting dynamic in an instructional unit, making inquiry permissible and imagination useful. Too often, instructional groups are burdened with the task of informational transfer without time for assimilation or application. It is better to value assimilation and acknowledge that learning happens best when the usefulness of information is readily perceived. This way new information can be integrated with previous knowledge. *The more a student understands the need for the information, the more the information is valued.*

Let's look at an example.

Monday morning at Crazy Times Junior High School:
The solar system is the science subject for the week. The students have received limited information about the planets of the solar system prior to this time. How do you, the teacher, incorporate the debriefing process into a discussion of the solar system? You begin by validating the relevance of studying the planets and the solar system.

Teacher:	Why should we study the planets and stars at all? They are all so far away and don't bother us.
Student:	Maybe there are people up there.
Teacher:	So?
Student:	Well, if there are people up there, we could go visit.
Teacher:	Do you think it would be possible for us to visit?
Student:	We went to the moon, didn't we?
Teacher:	Okay, so maybe we need to know about the planets in order to travel in space. Other reasons?
Student:	Other places might have fuel sources.
Teacher:	Great. So it is beneficial to know how each planet is made up. What might this knowledge have to offer us on Earth?

Possible summation:

Okay, let me see if I have got it all. We should study the solar system in case there are people or beings on other planets that we might want to communicate with and learn from and possibly visit. Other planets might have things that we need to keep Earth safe and—did I get it all? Oh, yes, other planets and stars might affect us in unexpected ways, and we should understand how in case of trouble. Good job. Now to the next step—what do we know already?

Hints for the Debriefing Process

Ask questions as if you need the answer. Make questions as personal as possible.

Play Columbo. Many kids view adults as out of touch, so play on that role: "Why do you suppose . . . ?" "I don't get it . . ." "Wait a minute, you mean to say you think . . ." "I am confused . . ."

Ask closed questions to establish agreement. How many of you think that the planets and stars directly affect our lives?

Paraphrase what you want to underscore. You are the filter. The information that you highlight and acknowledge becomes important.

Step 2: Make the information real

In Step 1, the group agrees to assess the validity of new information, including why it is important and how it relates to past, present, and future. Now the group explores ways to *act* on the information:

1. How does this information affect the quality of my life? In what areas might this information be important?

2. How can I improve an existing situation or reach an objective or goal as a result of this information?

3. If I took this information and combined it with another piece of information, what would I have created?

These three inquiries promote critical thinking and creatively help link cause and effect processes. Creative thinking is the making of something new and unique through the use of memory and prior learning. Creative thinking typically requires perspective from past experiences, prior learning, and the need for something new or different. The process of making the information real provides the foundation for higher order cognition and increased capabilities. Kids should be taught to *think*, and this process takes time, practice, and constant reframing.

At this phase of development the instructional group can begin to employ various interactional methods. Games, cooperative exercises, and role-playing are all well suited for this task. In the solar system lesson, for example, to have the students understand the usefulness of the information, the teacher could break the class into small cooperative groups. Each group is assigned a different planet and given the task of figuring out what a "space being" would look like, considering the physical characteristics of that planet (critical thinking). Perhaps students could figure out how to communicate with their space beings should they land on Earth (interpersonal sensitivity). Or maybe they could figure out how nonearthlings would save our planet from destructive pollutants (reflective and critical processes).

The best presentation of data entails all three basic learning styles: auditory, visual, and kinesthetic. Present the information so it can be heard, seen, and experienced.

Step 3: Apply the information

Step 1 seeks validation from kids that the information is perceived as valuable. Step 2 inventories the data so the kids can decide if the information is relevant to them. Step 3 asks the group to use the information in a variety of imaginative ways. While the techniques and tasks may vary, the thrust of this third step is to request the group to actually apply what has been assimilated.

Step 3 attempts to generalize the learning. The emphasis is on "doing." The group process is used to facilitate real and tangible productivity from lessons taught. Special ways to encourage greater understanding and application might include short story or poetry writing, lyric narration, artistry, making a video game, reporting the news, role-playing, simulations, cooperative ventures—the list is limitless.

In keeping with the earlier example, after the need for understanding the solar system is clear and the information is made real, the challenge to the teacher is to generalize the learning to everyday life. Perhaps students could be asked to write a short story about interplanetary travel, describing environmental conditions of each planet with special emphasis on survival of the inhabitants. Maybe students could be asked to imagine themselves as reporters for the *Galaxy News*. The current headline: "Planet Earth Has Designed a New Ecological Plan." What is the plan? Even a game of "Jeopardy" could be played using the information gleaned from the didactic information shared.

You are limited only by your own creativity. Generalizing the lessons taught anchors education to real life. Real-life applicability helps kids make sense of any course of study.

The instructional group is a vital tool in any classroom, aiding in the development of process skills like cooperation, collaboration, and compromise. Done well, the instructional group offers latitude for varied learning styles, aiding those who most need it in nonthreatening ways and providing an arena to learn about self while in a productive task.

Personal Awareness Groups

Personal awareness groups can increase personal insight and functioning. The group experience may foster positive life-style shifts.

As soon as you inquire about feelings in a group setting or seek self-disclosure, you are embarking upon an awareness group experience. As conceptualized, this is not a sensitivity session but an opportunity for kids to get in touch with their feelings and reactions to life events.

Too many kids are experiencing nonsupportive home environments; too few kids have adult role models who are accessible and available. Many kids live in homes where personal interactions are minimal, where they are provided with no more than a roof, clothes, and food. They never get to discuss their feelings and deal with their "what ifs" and "I'm scareds."

By the age of twelve, many of these kids are totally reliant on their peer group for the feedback and support they lack at home. This means that many kids are misinformed, ill-directed, and lack the basic information to constructively process the everyday stressors they encounter. We see this situation reflected in an increased rate of adolescent suicide, accident, assault, and psychiatric disorder.

We have learned that help for these kids can be as easy as providing the opportunity to talk in a safe and supportive environment. Somehow the burdens are lessened when they are shared. Awareness groups don't demand higher order counseling or clinical skills. Good listeners who don't try to fix or advise can make a major difference in many kids' lives. The goal of an awareness group is to provide a safe arena for disclosure, support, and nurturance. Such groups are nonprobing and nonthreatening.

Group leaders need to know a few basics to help them set boundaries. The first boundary concerns the limits of confidentiality. Caretakers are required to report imminent danger to a child, as well as any suspicion of child abuse or neglect. If a court subpoenas information, those who make reports are also required to divulge what they know. The second boundary is more subjective and requires insight on the part of group leaders: Adults need to seek help for any child who presents information, a demeanor, or problems outside their own range of experience.

The greatest nemesis of awareness groups is a leader who takes on too much, promises remedies, and is held hostage by secrets. Being held hostage by a secret is a product of a negative contract or agreement in a group. For example, Susan wants to tell the group something but asks that no one tell. A group agreement of this kind might have to be broken if Susan reports that she is somehow in danger. Federal law mandates reporting, so it is best not to agree to such a limitation. This keeps the process honest and offers the leader an avenue to express concern if need be. Students will still disclose in the face of these kinds of limitations.

As a leader, keep yourself out of the process. You are there to guide, facilitate, and gatekeep. You are not there to probe, fix, diagnose, or advise. On the next page you'll find some techniques ("Hints for the Awareness Group Process") for being involved while remaining professionally separate. These hints can serve you well in any setting where kids are asked to talk about themselves in terms other than the obvious and the superficial. Nothing has to be scary about incorporating this strategy into any work with kids. It is an effective way to discuss daily events, historical perspectives, and personal experiences.

Remember, awareness groups are not therapy groups. Psychotherapy is a skill-based, theoretically framed level of inquiry and analysis, and group therapy is a professionally guided process. Therefore, don't probe in an awareness group. Don't judge or analyze. Don't diagnose or advise. Don't assume you understand why. Don't pretend you can fix the problem.

A psychotherapist might say, "How did this reaction differ from other arguments you have had with your dad?" An awareness group leader might say, "Umm, I wonder if others have had to deal with this kind of an experience." The psychotherapist has a contract to probe. No such agreement exists among the members in an awareness group.

I can't help but recall a favorite scene from the movie *Crocodile Dundee*, when Dundee is introduced to a strange woman. His compan-

Hints for the
Awareness Group Process

Establish confidentiality as a norm.

In any group where self-disclosure is likely or integral to the overall process, confidentiality needs to be explained as a process that allows and protects personal disclosure. The only exceptions to the confidentiality rule are when a youth is at risk of imminent harm, when abuse or neglect is suspected, or when a court subpoenas information.

State the obvious: "What you see and hear in this room must stay here except in situations where someone might be in danger. I am bound by law to report youth in dangerous situations. Also, I may need help to work with this group effectively. I sometimes have to go outside of the group to get the information needed or to get help in creating a strategy to help someone in the group. I am bound by clear ethical guidelines. I need you to trust that I will honor confidentiality through any professional encounter. You may talk about your own experiences in this group, but you must not tell about others' problems and experiences. Other group members need to be assured of confidentiality. It is an important part of safety in this group."

Create rules to protect the integrity of the process.

For example:

> No put-downs.
>
> No threats.
>
> One person talks at a time.
>
> Feedback should be helpful.
>
> Come from a caring place.
>
> Speak for yourself.

Stay conscious of the process.

Are the efforts producing positive gains? If not, *stop the process.* It is never okay to sacrifice one group member for another. Kids have a tendency to judge one another harshly. *Run interference with scapegoating of any kind.* A good way to block scapegoating is to enforce a "speak for yourself" rule.

Don't carry the burden.

Group process is effective when the group spontaneously shares the leadership role. In other words, the quality of the group is the responsibility of all group members.

ion whispers that the woman sees a psychiatrist regularly. Dundee inquires, "What is a psychiatrist?" "Someone who listens and helps out when you get into trouble or are feeling sad." Dundee pauses, then says, "What's the matter? Ain't she got no mates?" Maybe if she had more "mates," she would feel better about her world. The awareness group provides "mates"; the psychotherapeutic group attempts to figure out why she ain't got no mates!

Some of the most effective awareness groups are guided by seeking answers to five basic questions:

1. What is your evidence?

2. What are the implications of this belief?

3. Are there alternative ways to view this situation?

4. What would be the benefit or gain?

5. What are you doing now that is working for you?

Let's explore: Take the case of Danny, a fifteen-year-old boy assigned to a dropout prevention group at school. Danny always talks in absolutes: "Nobody ever . . ." "I'll never . . ." "I don't need . . ." "So what. I don't care." His favorite retort is "Fine."

From the dialogue presented here, can you figure out which of the five basic questions the leader wants Danny to answer?

Leader: Danny, I don't get it. What's your evidence that Mr. Garcia picks on you?

Danny: He gives me dirty looks, and he hates me.

Leader: Hates you? What would he gain by hating you? What would be the benefit?

Danny: Fine! You don't have to believe me.

Leader: Danny, I do believe you. I just don't know if it's as cut and dried as you make it out to be. Could there be another way of looking at this situation? Are there explanations for Mr. Garcia's behavior other than "he hates me"?

Jake: (Another group member) I heard that Mr. Garcia's wife is sick—real sick. They say he's been weird ever since. Maybe that's why he seems to hate you—and besides, I think he's just weird.

Danny: So what. I don't care what you think.

Leader: Danny, is that fair? Everybody has the right to express themselves here.

Danny: I don't know how this got to be such a big deal. All I said was it doesn't seem to matter if you drop out 'cause most of the teachers don't care anyway.

Leader: I think it is a big deal because of what it implies. What would be the implications if this were a school where nobody cares?

Danny: I dunno. Maybe some people care. But not Mr. Garcia. He's just dumb. Maybe I am not in a good mood right now. Somebody else talk . . .

Obviously, this is a contrived example, but it underscores the way a leader can facilitate the dialogue. Here the leader is trying to get Danny to look at different ways to interpret Mr. Garcia's behavior. I keep these five questions constantly in mind as a part of my own filter system. They serve to check information and help a kid see another side or perspective.

Awareness groups vary in size, focus, and length. Charismatic leaders can carry large groups through this kind of a process. Most leaders need to restrict group size to between ten and twelve kids. However, don't let this estimate limit you. You'll be able to do most of what you set out to do if you follow three prep steps:

1. Know what the group members think about the experience they are about to share. Also, know their expectations.

2. Develop a contingency plan if everything you've prepared doesn't seem to work. Keep an ace up your sleeve. (My ace is the game "Do You Love Your Neighbor?"—see page 89. It always saves me.)

3. Focus on the positive, on the outcome, on future possibilities, and on having fun.

In most school settings the group experience will be limited to a single class period and eight to ten sessions. Plan accordingly. Less is better in group. If you plan too much and aren't able to finish, kids always feel ripped off. Keep group size, tasks, and expectations in line with the time allotment.

Remember, the leader is not responsible for what happens in the group, but the leader is responsible for setting up the process so that the group is facilitated well. A quick checklist might assist:

1. Do the kids understand confidentiality?

2. Is the room set up so that outside interruptions will be rare?

3. Are membership rules clear? Posted? Reviewed regularly?

4. Is the size conducive to the time allotted?

5. Are the kids appropriate for this type of group?

6. Do members feel safe enough to talk?

The awareness group is an excellent process to use to address many of the needs kids have. In a world that is less safe, less secure, and less predictable every year, kids need places where feelings can be acknowledged and expressed, where their perspectives are honored, and where condemnation is banned. They also need environments where they can try out new skills, receive feedback, and gain support and applause. For many kids, systems outside of the family and neighborhood will have to help if the kids are to be guided at all. Graduates of awareness groups say things like "Somebody was there for me," "Somebody listened," "I found out I am not alone," and "Maybe we are all more alike than different."

Skill-Building Groups

Skill-building groups are orchestrated to build a skills repertoire that can aid in reducing stress and increasing coping mechanisms. In our rapidly changing society, families have trouble coping. The community has too few resources and people seem preoccupied with economic survival. As helpers, we need to teach some of the more basic coping skills.

For example, a student who learns to go to the library to do homework after school instead of sitting at home watching TV alone is coping. Refusal skills are vital to a coping repertoire. Knowing how to assess possible danger, having the ability to withdraw from situations, and being able to ask for help are all aspects of coping. The greatest coping skill relies on the ability to develop relationships that matter to you. Allowing someone to be close to you is an extension of coping.

Coping is simply what you do to answer the real-life situations that you are dealt. Some coping strategies are positive and some can become negative. The barometer delineating the difference between positive and negative must be checked in the long run. For example, learning to withdraw from an alcoholic, abusive father may be a positive choice in some situations, but withdrawal from all adults is likely to be negative over time.

Our society seems to be in a downward spiral, a maelstrom. The spin is fed by shifts that our children are forced to reckon with on a daily basis:

1. an information and service-based age that has changed what people need to know

2. a technology that demands higher order skills from an ill-trained labor pool

3. a need to restructure and reorder our educational systems so that they respond more appropriately to the needs of the decade

4. family changes that have left many kids with unresolved emotional baggage and without available role models and safe places to talk

5. a poor understanding of how to help folks from diverse ethnic backgrounds

6. a society that does not view kids as community assets

7. a future that is unpredictable and daunting

When Hans Selye first coined the term "stress" in 1936, he probably never dreamed that the word would describe our current society.[4] Selye talked about stress as a stimulus of such severity that it causes disequilibrium. His definition always conjures an interesting image for me: a human figure bent at the waist, off balance.

The human condition is such that we always strive for homeostasis, to balance ourselves whenever we get off center. In the last twenty years, increased stress has fostered a proliferation of negative balancing mechanisms: alcohol and other drug abuse, child abuse, divorce, abandonment, and school dropout, to name just a few.

However, stress does not have to signify loss and destruction. Equilibrium can be achieved and health sustained through the use of coping mechanisms. As long as the scale between stressful life events and positive coping stays in balance, we can use stress to our advantage. For many, stress serves as a precursor to revving up for a challenge.

Approaching life situations as challenges is evidence of positive coping strategies. These coping strategies are a key to survival in modern society. They are an important part of everyone's repertoire; however, these coping skills are especially important for kids. Remember, things happen to kids, whereas adults manage what happens. This is an interesting—and important—distinction.

The development of coping mechanisms is vital to kids' survival. Kids seldom are in charge of what happens to them. This leaves them vulnerable to negative long-term effects when they face high-stress and high-risk experiences. They have to learn to balance or mitigate the impact of whatever happens. Perhaps we should prepare all kids for the worst case scenario in order to protect them the best. *Prevention rather than cure* becomes the task. Admittedly, it is an overwhelming task.

Stress management has no common or singular approach, so no generic "trick bag" can help you teach coping skills. Everyone responds uniquely to stress. One thing I have found helpful is to analyze coping strategies, which can be looked at in terms of skill levels.

Level 1: Concrete skills
These skills are easily understood and taught. The steps for acquisition are usually sequential and logical.

Level 2: Creative skills
These skills are creative and subtle. They are more difficult to describe because they do not follow logical guidelines. Level 2 skills seem to be the outcome or synthesis of an inner-directed process rather than a cognition or action.

Let's look at a scenario involving coping: Jenna is fifteen. She wants to be popular, and she wants to fit in with the fast-paced crowd at school. She goes to a party with a group of girls from the "popular" group. When she arrives, she is hopeful (creative skill) that this will be a great evening. One of the girls encourages her to have a beer, but she refuses (concrete skill). She decides (concrete skill) to call home and ask for a ride (concrete skill). Her mom picks her up at the party. While talking to her mom, she is able to articulate her insight (creative skill) that she doesn't need to belong to the popular group. She is able to forecast optimistically (creative skill) about the new situations she will encounter. She talks herself into gaining perspective.

We all engage in self-talk or inner dialogue, a basic position from which we judge the world. This inner process, in turn, often seems to direct the kind of coping techniques we will select. If we as helpers of kids can encourage this inner dialogue, we can increase the positive coping strategies an individual uses. For most people, this inner dialogue will be constructive and self-enhancing. For a few it will be negative and potentially self-destructive. To be helpful to children, an adult helper needs to ask the essential question: "Is this coping technique working for you or against you?"

To determine whether a coping mechanism is positive or negative, closely examine the impact it has. A positive coping strategy has beneficial effects in both the short and the long term. For example, playing racquetball after school is likely to provide long-term stress reduction, along with other positive health benefits. Getting drunk after a bad day may temporarily relieve current stress, but getting drunk frequently is counterproductive, and its consequences ultimately add to the level of stress.

Having multiple strategies makes coping easier. When one strategy does not work, you can try another. The more techniques available, the better the chance one has of responding positively.

Coping Strategies

Level 1: Concrete skills

Asks for help
Organizes well
Solves problems
Can make decisions
Plans and forecasts
Is able to participate
Is socially competent
Has a sense of humor
Delays gratification
Knows what is real
Has refusal skills

Level 2: Creative skills

Is able to "let go"
Believes in a higher power
Believes in personal efficacy
Thinks abstractly
Is optimistic
Has a sense of belonging
Is able to care for others
Plays well
Is sensitive to others
Avoids blame or shame games
Has the ability to distance self

This listing is distilled from the research efforts of Norman Garmezy and E. James Anthony, who are interested in the nature and development of personal competency arising despite stressful histories.[5] While tabloid journalists would have us believe that the experiences of our childhood can become the burden of a lifetime, Garmezy and Anthony challenge us to learn to cope better and let go.

"Letting go" is a tough concept to define but an important concept to grasp. Letting go refers to that process when an individual decides not to give power to a given situation or condition. It describes a freeing from pain or situations that have become burdensome. Letting go sometimes is the step needed to go on with life after some trauma.

Maybe examples will help: The incest survivor lets go of the pain in order to continue in the world of relationships. She does not forget; she stops giving the memory of the incest the power to control her life. The accident victim has to let go and accept his physical disability before he can really recuperate. The parent has to let go of blaming herself when her son needs rehabilitation for addiction. The student has to let go of her dream to go to Stanford University when she is not accepted. Letting go and moving on are skills necessary for real coping in today's world.

The following guidelines provide a framework for the beginning stage of coping skills development:

1. Create a menu of skills and provide choices. Don't impose solutions.

2. Concentrate on developing skills consistent with personal beliefs and values. Let the kids know they have a responsibility to walk their talk—in other words, to act on their beliefs.

3. Be open to trying new options or methods. Invent alternatives.

4. Pay attention to the most immediate needs first.

5. Declare any boundaries that may exist. State any nonnegotiables.

You'll find it easier to start with the concrete skills because kids receive more immediate feedback and therefore achieve some success more quickly. As with imparting information, teaching concrete skills is like teaching someone to dance. Step one, two, three—cha-cha-cha. For example, if the skill is "asking for help," proceed with the six essential steps.

Step 1: Perceive the need

Why is this skill important to the quality of life?

Step 2: Formulate a rationale

How will the skill be used?

Step 3: Check for alternates and select a strategy

Study the various methods and choose which is most appropriate

Step 4: Practice the process

Create a vignette and role-play. Ask the students in your group to practice asking for help from various people (mother, teacher, best friend, sales clerk).

Step 5: Review for personal insight

Following the practice, reflect upon any information that became obvious to you about the students' ability to ask for help.

Step 6: Teach the skill

Try to reduce or eliminate any perceived barriers to the effective use of this skill. Then ask the students to teach the skill to someone else.

The first, second, and third steps in teaching each concrete skill may differ, but the fourth, fifth, and sixth steps remain constant. For example, for three different concrete skills—organization, problem solving, and decision making—the first three steps to learn are as follows:

Organization:
1. Assess the situation.
2. Sort the information.
3. Categorize the data.

Problem solving:
1. Invent alternatives.
2. Review options.
3. Predict outcomes.

Decision making:
1. Weigh alternatives.
2. Select alternative.
3. Forecast success.
4. Take action.

The last three steps for teaching all three of these concrete skills remain the same: practice, review, and teach the skill. The very best way to acquire a skill is to be responsible for teaching it.

This is not a complicated system. Kids like to figure out for themselves what might work. A word of caution: *Concrete skill building may or may not lead to creative skill acquisition.*

Creative skills are more powerful than concrete skills, and they are more likely to generate greater long-term effects. However, creative skills are more difficult to teach than are skills framed by cognition and specific behavior. Creative skills are in some ways a synthesis and extension of concrete skills, but they are not necessarily acquired in a sequential format. Most often, these lessons are assimilated from personal experiences. The process is idiosyncratic. Some people seem to be born with some of these creative skills, while others learn them through an evoking experience. A few people may never need or acquire creative-based skills.

The group process can be used effectively to provide the opportunity for both levels of skill acquisition. For example:

The dilemma:

Organize a group of high school sophomores into groups of eight. Tell the kids that the United States plans to establish the first small colony on Mars, to be composed of twelve carefully selected individuals. The colony is expected to remain in place for a minimum of fifteen years. Ask each group to select the twelve individuals and to tell why they chose who they did.

The group begins. Values and mores are explored. What is practical? What makes the most sense? This is a complex skills challenge. You can create even more drama by assigning role scripts to selected individuals within the group. Now each member has to argue personal worth and value according to scripted boundaries.

The group process provides a feedback loop, a variety of perceptions, and a chance to practice techniques with safety. The process of building a repertoire of coping skills can be promoted well within the context of the group. Some of the best ways to do this are simulations, games, role-playing, and investigative interviews. The classroom, too, can become a laboratory for developing coping skills, even when teaching focuses on an entirely different content area. Some examples follow.

English composition:

Divide students into groups of three. Ask each group to select three local citizens they respect. For each citizen chosen, the students must conduct an interview and then chronicle the individual's life history. Ask students to pay special attention to each individual's personal coping methods. Finally, the group must compare the coping strategies used by each of the three individuals, then compare the coping skills of those interviewed with their own personal coping strategies.

Art:

Everyone receives one piece of paper—same size, same color. Each student folds the paper into a flower. Examine and applaud the differences. There are, of course, many solutions to a single problem.

History:

Topic for discussion and/or research: Which political figures in the last century are noted for exhibiting poor coping mechanisms? Who are they, and how were these negative strategies handled by their peers?

These three activities are designed to complement an existing lesson plan. They encourage critical thinking about coping processes. If schools are to address the needs of their students, they must integrate coping mechanisms into curricula. Teaching coping and survival skills does not require course content change, but it does require a change in teaching methodology.

Chapter 3 delves deeper into coping skills and strategies. A number of activities are presented that use group dynamics to emphasize significant teaching points. These activities can be applied in the many settings where kids gather.

NOTES

1. Bruce W. Tuckman and Mary Ann C. Jensen, "Stages of Small Group Development Revisited," *Group and Organization Studies* 2 (1977).

2. Steve Zuieback, 1992. Unpublished material, reprinted by permission of the author.

3. Marion Haynes, *Effective Meeting Skills: A Practical Guide for More Productive Meetings* (Menlo Park, CA: Crisp Publications, 1988), 30.

4. Hans Selye, "History and Present Status of the Stress Concept," in *Handbook of Stress: Theoretical and Clinical Aspects,* eds. Leo Goldberger and Schlomo Breznitz (New York: Free Press, 1982).

5. For specific works by Norman Garmezy and E. James Anthony, see the bibliography.

CHAPTER 3

Managing Change and Making Connections with Kids

HELPING KIDS TO SUCCEED depends on your ability to connect with kids. "Connecting" requires spanning generational inequalities in innovative ways to make it safe to have genuine interaction. Games, play, and laughter make some of the best generational links. Once the bridges are established, the opportunity exists to develop a level of intimacy. Once a sense of intimacy or closeness exists, influence becomes possible. But intimacy and influence are not inherent within interactional processes. First you have to get the kids' attention. Play helps create arenas where relationships can be built. One child named Craig described the feeling of being overlooked:

> It is six months into the school year. Yet each day you watch me play alone at recess. I play beside other kids, but I play alone. No one picks me. They ignore me when I approach. You feel sorry for me, I know. But you are the teacher—the Creator of Games. They listen to you; they obey you. Can't you make it a game to figure out how to include me? You are the only person strong enough to make them stop and see who I am.[1]

I wish Craig were the only child waiting in the wings for adult intervention. Unfortunately, more children are waiting than are served. Somehow we have to shift our thinking about the role we play in organizing and facilitating the classroom group. I prefer to think of myself as a guide, a gatekeeper, and a facilitator. In these terms, my job is to create the arena for equal opportunity to learn. Each child must be embraced as a unique learner—equal but not the same.

All adults will be challenged to reckon with this role shift during this decade. Parents and teachers alike are struggling with this great societal movement, this rapid change that has left most of us without a pertinent reference point for response. The world is different—but kids are not different. Growing up still takes time, kids' needs still motivate their behavior, and negative acting out still provides benefits.

As caregivers, our job has changed and requires new strategies for our connections with kids to be meaningful and influential. Managing change is the tough part. If (to borrow a metaphor from Ray Golarz, superintendent of Richmond, Indiana, Community Schools) schools are like fish tanks, then new filters are required and the water needs to be changed. Higher standards for ongoing care are necessary.

But are schools like fish tanks? Many aspects are similar:

The environment is greatly affected by the inhabitants.

The harmonious interaction among all members of the environment is essential, or danger may exist for some.

Each member of the system is unique and contributes at some level.

No one member has total control.

All kinds of living things are needed to create a viable environment.

Change is inevitable; without change the system risks extinction.

Change requires outside help.

The major problem for both schools and fish tanks is identifying who is responsible for change. Until responsibility for change is assigned or assumed, the fish in the tank will continue to suffer.

In the case of schools, identifying those responsible for change has resulted in a lot of shaming, a lot of blaming, and very little aiming. As educators we know what needs to be done, and we have the ability to bring about change. Unfortunately, understanding the need and having the capacity for change are not guarantees of action.

As has become apparent from my own observation and from dialogues with those in the midst of the change process, the greatest barriers to effective change in education seem to be:

1. commitment to change as a process ("I want too much too soon")

2. differing views of the process by those involved ("I can see the need to change and the possible results of change only through my personal filters")

3. the fear of starting over from the beginning ("It's easier to stay the same")

I have come to liken change to the addiction recovery process: Both require a real shift in behavior and new filters from which to gain perspective. Look at the chart on page 58 ("Recovery: A Metaphor for Change") to see if the comparison fits.

Perhaps comparing the change process to addiction recovery seems a bit harsh, but it really isn't so farfetched. A habit is a habit is a habit. Desire must undeniably precede any difficult endeavor, and teacher change is very difficult. I am challenging you to shift from an adult-centered process to a kid-centered one, and I am guaranteeing that moving toward a kid-centered focus will result in positive gains in the classroom environment and the kids' learning. All you have to do is "let go" and integrate fun into the curriculum. Don't miss out on this important opportunity.

Rules for Making Connections with Kids

1. Get their attention.

2. Make sense of what you offer.

3. Send clear messages.

4. Be congruent or acknowledge the incongruities.
   Walk your talk and speak to any obvious departures from what you say.

5. Speak to the obvious; tell the truth.

Most kids really like to be with adults who allow themselves to "let go" and truly have fun. For many kids the benchmarks of true fun are laughter and taking a chance. I have seen the best lessons taught while talking about an activity, experience, or situation that caused a belly laugh. Done well, the experience is remembered and helps ease the next encounter.

The trick is to turn the game into an experience, wrap the lesson around the play, and then talk about the teaching points—all in the spirit of fun. For example, to underscore the insidiousness of peer pressure, I might ask the group to play a quick round of "body parts" (a disguised "head, shoulders, knees, and toes" borrowed from preschool). Kids and adults alike will usually say they are too old to play such a game. They resist from the outset. Set them up to *do* rather than to talk about doing. Say, "When I call out a body part, I want you to touch it with both hands. You may touch *only* your own parts. Now: head, shoulders, knees and toes, knees and toes."

After establishing the rhythm, I begin to model touching the named body part with the group. Once I notice that they are following me, I will call out "shoulders" and I will touch my head. A majority of those in the group will also touch their heads.

Recovery: A Metaphor for Change

For the addict

Preconscious stage:

At this stage the addict is becoming uncomfortable and is having difficulty rationalizing what is happening. Denial is normal and delusion likely. Typically, the addict seeks out external sources to blame and will solicit coalitions to validate positions.

Conscious stage:

The addict now knows why the life problems exist but is unwilling to acknowledge the ability to take control. Shame and blame become norms. Loss becomes evident. Excuses are less and less viable, and evidence is clear that something needs to happen.

Experimental stage:

At this point, the addict attempts to fix the problem: quick fixes, easy shifts in behavior, attempts to prove that the perspective is accurate. Subtly, a shift has occurred from thinking and cognition to action. Once action starts, it becomes difficult to return to the stage in which denial works. The addict will never "use" comfortably again.

Relapse stage:

Relapse is normal and can be productive. It sometimes serves as the stepping-stone to commitment for change. Management of change requires positive responses to the propensity to return to the familiar.

Commitment or sacrifice stage:

Change is commitment. Commitment is willingness driven by forthcoming action. At some point, the addict must choose recovery with a change contract or be sacrificed to the addiction process. No one can gauge for another when enough is enough. Everyone comes to this choice alone.

For the educator

Are my methods working the same way they used to?

Are my responses appropriate?

Do the kids like my class?

How can I do this differently?

Why is this happening?

What needs to be done?

How can I build success for all?

If all kids can learn, how can I ensure positive effort?

Who shares this burden?

I'll do it my way!

They should change!

Was I wrong before?

The kids need it.

Change will create better strategies.

. . . or . . .

I'll wait until they mandate it.

Now for the wrapping: "What happened just now is like peer pressure. Without cognition—thinking—people will follow. They do this even when they have had prior experience, even when they know better." This activity is a great opener to a dialogue about peer pressure. The point is easily made that kids need more than just wishing to say no. The lesson is "wrapped" around the play.

This method of teaching has significant payoffs. The lessons become more relevant and better understood. Kids take more ownership for the learning because they are part of the process and the process becomes part of them. They may associate you with the activity and reexperience the feelings assigned to the activity when they encounter you, but the integrated learning is their own.

Owning the lesson is the key to a future of lifelong learning. Enticing children to become thoughtful will serve them forever more. Einstein is purported to have said, "The purpose of education is to nurture thoughtfulness. The lesser function of thinking is to solve problems and puzzles. The essential purpose is to decide for oneself what is of value in life, and then to find the courage to take your own thoughts seriously."[2] As educators our job is to nurture and facilitate thinking. The priorities in education can reflect this bias, according to Lynn Stoddard, who offers the following as things we must do:[3]

1. Help children develop their talents and feelings as members of the great human family.

2. Help children develop their powers of communication and expression.

3. Help children develop their inquiring, creative minds.

I think these ideas can be simply stated: *Set up your lessons so children succeed.* Student success can be accomplished in a variety of ways; it will most certainly result from the integration of multiple learning styles, a cooperative process, and lessons that are individually tailored anchors to real life. Following are some concrete examples of what I mean.

When asked to take over a lesson that involved teaching fifth graders about the solar system, I was challenged to bring a really diverse group together. I even had a side bet with the teacher that if she would create the test, I would conduct the lessons. I forecasted that the process would make a difference in what the kids learned and that the evidence would be higher than average scores on a test that she developed!

The first thing I did was tell the kids about a trip to Europe, an adventure when I was young that allowed me to visit and explore the quarries where Michelangelo acquired his sculpting materials. We talked about travel, transportation, and space—*informally.* The next step was to discuss Michelangelo's methods during the painting of the Sistine Chapel—backbreaking labor on scaffolds, painting small areas, one at a time.

Then we looked at a picture of the solar system. We made a grid, assigned areas for development, and the kids worked on their backs—about an hour a day for three days—putting the solar system in place on the ceiling of the classroom. Only after finishing our ceiling work did we begin to describe each planet.

I broke the kids into cooperative groups and assigned each group one planet to build. All the planets were then assimilated into the solar system, this time 3-D style. Together we fantasized about what space beings might look like, and then we created our own outer space aliens based on what we knew about the planets. We created a language for each planet, then planned an intergalactic party.

Three debriefing questions were used in this process:

What surprised you?

Why is this information important?

How will you use this information?

Students were encouraged to become experts in the process. Some became involved in the artistic process of creating the solar system while others focused on specific facts. Still others took responsibility for getting the materials needed. Throughout the process I was especially impressed by the kids, who were really invested in one another's success.

All learning styles were utilized, and the process allowed for varied role exploration as well as for varied group experiences. When the kids took the test prepared by the classroom teacher, no one scored less than 82 percent. We all felt like celebrating. Not only did the kids glean new information, but they were able to use the information and have it make sense in their world. We played, we learned, and we had fun.

Another example: I am known as the "Fart Lady" to a lot of kids. Why? Because I often open with a monologue about my concerns about cow farts and the effect of methane gas on the ozone layer. (Yes, it's true. Cow farts and belches are great pollutants. I have actually had to add "belches" because recent news reports indicate the ozone layer is more threatened by cow belches than cow farts!)

While I talk about farts, I do some investigating of my audience: "How many of you fart? Dr. Dean Edell [a TV doctor] claims that the average person farts about twenty times a day. How many of you fart that often?"

After the discussion focusing on farts, we might discuss why we laugh when we talk about farts, or we might start a dialogue about needing alternative sources of energy. With either emphasis, something important has happened. The kids are talking *with* an adult. The playful conversation made it safe and fun, if not plain funny. They'll remember their reactions and feelings.

Try the ideas and play the games in this book to engage kids in your life. These activities can become part of a classroom lesson, a family outing, or a special retreat. All of the games build relationships. Many games kids play focus on competition and being the best, the winner—

not these. Rather, these activities make everybody a winner. The wrapping applications—the lessons that wrap around the games—are limited only by your imagination.

Some precautions should be taken by anyone who becomes a facilitator of these activities.

1. Pay attention to the age range assigned to each activity.

As a rule of thumb, assume that the high and low ends of the scale will need special attention. For example, many eleven-year-old boys will have a hard time playing games that require touching one another or girls. Establishing rapport and cohesion before the activity won't help, either. You can't expect eleven-year-old boys to engage in touching to build rapport and cohesion. Likewise, older kids will often resist activities that seem juvenile to them. The key is to look for the appropriate moment when you can weave a particular activity into your lesson, and grasping that moment will depend on the experiences you are having with the group.

2. Do not expect your experience to generalize from one group to another.

Each group has a culture and a life all its own. The group process must be assessed to check for appropriate responses. If the activity isn't a good fit for the group, it loses its teaching utility. Don't be afraid to pull out of an activity that isn't working. If something isn't working, go on to something that will.

How do you know a good fit? Here are some hints.

The activity should match you.
This hint really refers to your ability to pull off the activity in a congruent and fun manner. I have seen facilitators blame an activity for not achieving a given goal when it was actually the way the facilitator introduced the process that led to its failure. Don't use language that would in any way reflect that *you* think the activity is too hard, too dumb, or too weird. The kids will mirror you.

The activity should match the abilities of the participants.
For example, when playing "Do You Love Your Neighbor?" (see page 89) with young kids, you should use noticeable physical traits in the activity; the older the group, the more abstract and feeling focused the characteristics can be.

The activity should match the participants' willingness to take risks and self-disclose.
If members of the group are unwilling to share personal information because they don't trust one another, then use activities that will build trust.

*The activity needs to match your intentions
for the group.*
Use only activities that are consistent with the theme or
focus being emphasized. Keep the order, keep the focus,
and keep up the involvement.

The activity must match the process.
The flow of activities must be interesting and match the
energy level of the group. For example, a group that has
just finished a fun, mobile, energetic game will need to
cool down before getting back to work. Likewise, a group
that has just spent an hour sharing personal information
may need a quick and energizing game. Think about
what you want to accomplish and match the activity
with your objectives. This process is a lot like dancing:
Anticipate the next step, listen to the tone, apologize and
keep going when the process isn't working.

3. Work to build cohesion as a consequence of positive interaction.

If the interaction is positive, trust evolves and cohesion is enhanced.
I like to use a model for cohesion that incorporates two major areas of
interactive dynamics: content and process. *Content* is *what* we say and
do, while *process* is *how* we say and do it. Low cohesion is based on
content-focused interactions, while high cohesion relies on the process
focus. As cohesion builds, members shift from a focus on "I" or "me" to
a focus on *belonging* ("we") and then *membership* ("it"). This shift from
"me" to "we" is a product of trust and an indicator of group cohesion.

4. Link effort to a long-term commitment to learning.

As educators we need to foster learning as a life-style. For children to be
truly prepared for their future, learning must become a norm, or they
will risk knowing how to do something that no longer needs to be done.
Every lesson needs to validate the process of learning. Every interaction,
every pondered idea, every experience can feed the learning process.

Most of the activities described in this book require low to
medium cohesion, so they can be used in most settings. High cohesion
is usually seen in ongoing groups. Don't expect to achieve a high level of
intimacy quickly or during one-time meetings.

The actual facilitation of the activities varies from group to group
and from activity to activity. Some basic rules of group dynamics must
be employed to establish and maintain a safe and ethically sound environment for the activities:

1. Every facilitator must recognize that any orchestrated
   interaction among people has the potential to uncover
   pain and personal difficulty. Be prepared to handle
   pain; *don't create it*. A good group experience does not

rely on tears or troubled interaction. Protect the integrity of each individual at all costs. Offer all participants the right to pass, to withhold comment. The process is not set up as a therapeutic experience; even if you are a therapist, you do not have a contract to probe or analyze. One quick way to check your direction is to ask yourself, "Am I trying to fix?" If you are *fixing*, *advising*, or *analyzing*, you have overstepped the acceptable boundaries of this kind of activity.

2. Make sure that any activity based on self-disclosure is preceded by a discussion about confidentiality. At the outset I always state the following: "What you hear and see here stays here. However, if I perceive someone in danger, I am bound by law to report that danger to authorities. A dangerous situation might be information about physical abuse, neglect, or menace. I have to make the decision. This is not negotiable."

3. Ask open-ended questions to process the group's experience. Repeat all answers and validate that you heard the comment. Make the comments fit. No put-downs. *Kids' insights, like their feelings, must always be validated.* Ask students whom you think to be in error to substantiate their case more thoroughly. Check for incongruities and possible logical pitfalls. Remember, differing opinions are okay.

4. Summarize the content of the insights disclosed. Make your teaching point overlap the disclosure and experience of the group members.

5. Give verbal feedback and acknowledge the effort of those trying to link the activity with life lessons. Notice their work and praise them.

6. Bring it back around—debrief. Reiterate the process by walking everyone through your experience of what happened. The debriefing helps to underscore the teaching points while focusing attention on the accomplishment achieved in completing the task. *Every activity needs to be debriefed.* Use "we" to boost inclusion. (For example, you might say, "Gosh, I had no idea when we started that we would gain so much by doing this activity. We really did a nice job. Now the task is to make what happened here make sense in the world. What made it easy? How did you work together? What happened here that might help you in your classes at school?") *Generalize the experience to something real and tangible in group members' lives.* Leave the activity after you have established that the process was worthwhile.

THE PROCESS OF DEBRIEFING

Making lessons tangible and realistic is perhaps the greatest challenge facing the adult facilitator. An adept leader can use any interaction to underscore significant lessons or enhance skills. *The trick is not the activity, but how the activity is used.* Any given activity can be debriefed in four different ways. This provides variety and dimension to the activity. Imagine . . .

> ***Sixth-grade classroom:***
> While studying Native Americans, the students are introduced to the idea of a totem pole. They are asked to construct a totem pole that illustrates the positive individual characteristics for each member in the cooperative group. (See "Team Totem" on page 140 for a variation on this idea.)

Debriefing 1: Process

How was it to work cooperatively?

What were the major roadblocks to getting your job done?

What would you do differently next time?

The process debriefing focuses on *how* the group or individual worked. The steps in problem solving are emphasized, thereby uncovering glitches in strategy and planning. Process debriefing is best used when the lessons to be highlighted are a product of human interaction.

Debriefing 2: Introspection

Did anyone find it tough to talk about positive attributes?

What gets in our way of talking about ourselves in positive terms?

What are the advantages of putting ourselves down?

What do you think when you hear people saying that they are good at something?

When debriefing for personal introspection, the facilitator has to be open to whatever is realized from the activity. The ability to glean insight varies in adolescence. No matter what the insight, the individual must be validated. Often this is a good time to ask questions like "What is your evidence?" and "If you believe . . . then what are the implications for you?"

Debriefing 3: Didactic applicability

What was going on in the Native American culture that made totem poles so important?

Why were they used?

What do we do in modern society to achieve the same goals? What and where are these modern-day totem poles?

This is the classic classroom form of debriefing. The didactic content of the lesson becomes fodder for other levels of inquiry in the same context. This type of debriefing needs to "bring the lesson home"—that is, make it applicable to the students' current experience. Generalizing the didactic to what is real makes the information more tangible and provides an answer to the age-old question "Why do I have to know this?"

Debriefing 4: Skills

What was the hardest part of this assignment?

What skills did you need in order to be successful?

What did you do that worked best?

What did you see others do that contributed to the overall success of the project?

So often kids assume that they are without skills and resources, that the world is too big and too full of pressure. The skills debriefing is designed to break through the "I can't" and the "I don't know how." Done well, skills debriefing will result in "I can" and "I do."

How does this work? Given an activity, kids will tap into skills they possess without thinking. The facilitator helps to identify the skills needed to accomplish the task and serves as a mirror to demonstrate that the skills were used in completing the task assigned. For most kids, doing becomes a way to understand competence and a vehicle to catalog a skills repertoire.

The debriefing process is vital in a creative classroom. Without debriefing, the activities seem to be done *to* students, rather than being *in service* to the students. The better the debriefing and the more often the process is reiterated, the better critical thinking skills are enhanced. In fact, debriefing is sorting information to glean content and reference. Debriefing is not a complicated process, but its success does rely on your ability to forecast and strategize. Remember that every human interaction has an inherent message—even if only "It is fun to act weird."

OVERCOMING BARRIERS TO PLAYFUL INTERACTION

Adults working with kids often raise two issues—or barriers—when presented with the beneficial use of "games":

1. "I don't want to do 'touchy-feely.'"

2. "I don't know how to play."

Let's look at both of these barriers.

Touchy-Feely

During the 1960s, a lot of helpers breached ethical boundaries in search of "meaning and truth." The invalid assumption was that the greater the personal exposure and the greater the pain, the more forthcoming the insight. Sometimes exacerbated by the use of drugs, the sixties' strategies too often undermined the esteem and hope they were alleged to support.

"Touchy-feely" is not a part of these activities, nor of the debriefing process. Feelings shared are important if insight and intimacy are to occur. However, a facilitator must not create pain for participants in the hope of some gain. For our purposes, the following cautions should be heeded:

1. *Never push for disclosure.* Forcing disclosure is unfair and outside of the context of any agreement in a classroom setting.

2. *Don't use put-downs to elicit a response.* Put-downs are always put-downs. No matter how you couch the experience, lessons learned in contrived pain are always tainted by the pain.

3. *Never intentionally hurt someone's feelings.* Having to respond to a painful emotional experience makes it tough for kids to *win.* Bolster the ego; don't tear it down. *Never create pain.*

4. *Don't push known buttons.* Even if you have prior knowledge of a situation or scenario, it is unfair to use such information.

5. *Never pretend to understand.* Be congruent and speak only in honest terms. Don't feign concern.

Honoring these five cautions will help protect the kids in the process of personal disclosure. These cautions also set boundaries and provide guidelines for interaction.

You will always manage emotion in facilitating activities with others—whether kids or adults. However, these guidelines ensure that the student is not being manipulated to disclose prematurely. Every individual's right to privacy should be upheld.

"I Don't Know How to Play"

I define play as interaction that is enjoyable and that may be accompanied by laughter. Play is not stand-up comedy. Play is not survival-camp duty. Play is not climbing ropes 150 feet in the air. Play could be all of these things or none of them. *Play* is your beliefs, your skills, and your style of interaction—all wrapped into a unique and idiosyncratic *you.*

You are the instrument and vehicle for play. How you behave becomes your personalized regime for play. Your personal "shtick" is your avenue to capture your audience. The barrier here is not that you don't know how to play but that you don't understand how to use your shtick. You may not even know you have a shtick.

Jack Benny had a shtick:

1. He was a miser.

2. He refused to admit to age beyond 39.

3. He had an interesting relationship with Rochester.

4. He played the violin. He wasn't very good, but he thought he was very, very good.

Jack Benny appealed to a wide range of people because he offered so many ways to connect with him. I liked him because of the violin, my mother understood his age thing, my dad liked the miserliness, and we *all* liked Rochester.

Not everyone has as broad a repertoire as Jack Benny, but we all have a shtick. Your shtick is the manifestation of your interests, passions, reality, and skills. The trick is to learn to use it.

My shtick incorporates a diverse set of circumstances: I use my love for being a mom and my career as a counselor to explain my passion for helping schools. I also like to read and understand "stuff," and I know that education is a vital asset for survival. In reality, I had a tough time fitting in at school, made a lot of bad decisions, and really needed help to survive. Somehow I learned to laugh, and I learned to be a friend. Charlie Chaplin once described humor as playing with pain. I have used play and humor to balance the stress and adversity of my life. These skills saved my life and are forever more a part of how I embrace the world—in other words, my shtick.

When folks meet me, they may meet any part of the whole that is me. They embrace what they need, like, or find interesting, and *that* becomes the point of initiation for our relationship. Likewise, when I embrace them I make a connection with some unique characteristic that is theirs. The relationship now has reciprocity. Now, we're cooking.

The chart on page 68 ("Shtick Mapping") can help you begin to identify what is idiosyncratically you.

The play process is not designed to manufacture a generic teacher, helper, or parent who plays with kids by using a set of prescribed activities. Rather, the goal is to help adults find out how they can best relate to kids, to be a part of their solutions to problems rather than a part of their problems. Methods that rely on attraction rather than promotion will be most successful.

Simply telling a kid to have a relationship with an adult is not enough to make it happen, but you can attract kids to you through your shtick and then work on establishing a relationship. From attraction, rapport is possible. Rapport is simply the "aliveness" of an interaction. With rapport, permission is gained. Permission describes a relationship where consent has been established. Finally, from permission influence occurs. A relationship of influence is what helps people "do."

Shtick Mapping

Interests	Passions
I am unique because:	I am driven to:
As a consequence, I do:	I am willing to help when:

Skills	Reality
I am capable of:	I am:
Things I do really well:	I need:
Things I like to do with others:	I want:
What I need to be better:	If only:

Connections

People connect with me when I:

I like people to know I:

My shtick is:

Once you become attractive, once a connection is made, the potential for a relationship of influence is heightened. Influence becomes an attribute of positive interactions. Adults *with* influence engage kids. Teachers, parents, and clergy *without* influence say "do" and "don't" a lot. The differences are remarkable.

With influence	Without influence
caring	guilting
nurturing	invading
giving feedback	criticizing
valuing	putting down
hoping	directing
guiding	ordering
goal setting	commanding
visioning	consuming
encouraging	expecting
respecting	blaming

It is sometimes useful to ask yourself, "How would the kids in my life characterize me? With or without influence?" How would you judge yourself?

RESILIENCY RESEARCH

Michael Rutter, a psychiatrist from London, England, studied kids in tough situations, usually associated with chronic pain and psychopathology. He found that a small percentage of these kids were able to navigate in the world without profound long-term difficulty, regardless of how horrendous the situation at home.[4] As long as these kids balanced the stress of the situation with adequate coping, they were able to remain productive. They survived, were resilient, and seemed invulnerable.

Two truisms emerge in the literature regarding the interrelationships between stress and risk:

1. Everybody reacts differently to stressful conditions; some adapt well and some adapt poorly.

2. Nobody can handle a plate that is too full for too long. Something has to be done to reduce high-level stress that is chronically experienced.

Risk and stress are best balanced by coping skills or the removal of the stress factors themselves. Julius Segal tells us that the risk/stress syndrome can be impacted through protective factors, which he defines as traits or conditions that mitigate—or even reverse—the child's at-risk status.[5] Norman Garmezy also writes of the mitigation of risk as a protective phenomenon.[6] He has highlighted six areas of competence that make functioning more likely:

1. effectiveness in work, play, and love

2. healthy expectancies and a positive outlook

3. high self-esteem and an internal locus of control (self-talk that assumes personal responsibility for one's actions, mores, and beliefs)

4. self-discipline

5. critical thinking skills

6. a sense of humor

Garmezy groups these protective factors into three categories: personal attributes, social milieu, and family traits. (See "Protective Factor Domains" below.[7]) Although having a high degree of competence in these three domains does not "fix" stress, it can help kids sustain adaptation and functioning. Knowing about these protective factors can also give us some direction in helping kids who are under stress strategize productively.

Protective Factor Domains

Personal attributes	Social milieu	Family traits

Good self-concept, self-esteem	Well-developed, accessible	Well-balanced approach to discipline
Interpersonal sensitivity	Supportive system	Consistently enforced rules
Cooperative, socially responsive	Positive school experience	Warm, close relationships
Sense of humor	Good quality schooling	Respect for individuality
Willing to delay gratification	Scope of opportunities	Respect for authority
Good communication skills	Good adult role model	Healthy communication patterns
Reflective, flexible	Fewer stressful life events	Supportive of outside social contacts
Impulse control	Informally available friends, teachers, significant others	
Future orientation		

Given their protective value, it makes sense for us to focus our efforts to teach communication, critical thinking, and social interaction skills on all three domains. These three areas are the foundation of positive self-esteem. Why? Because self-esteem is enhanced when you perceive yourself as competent and capable, as safe and having some control over your life. What better way to build self-regard than to be able to clearly represent yourself, ponder, and problem solve, while having good relationships?

E. James Anthony and Bertram Cohler offer another dimension to resiliency.[8] The three characteristics of resiliency they describe are:

1. confidence

2. the ability to distance self

3. the ability to resist pressure

These characteristics describe the skill arenas for helping kids make lifestyle choices; they are vital to refusal skills.

The chart on page 72, "Traits of the Resilient Child," gives an overview of the characteristics of resiliency identified by four resiliency researchers.[9]

The beliefs of resilient kids reflect an optimistic outlook, an anticipation of the future. This optimistic mind-set can also serve to buffer risk and stress. The beliefs of a resilient kid might sound like this:

I can handle it.

I am the master of my own fate.

I can figure out solutions to
my problems.

I am not alone.

People care about me.

I make a difference in the world.

For some kids, relearning or acquiring coping skills has meant letting go of helplessness and shifting from pessimism to optimism. New research indicates that optimism can be taught. For kids, this mandates good adult role models and a change in thinking, communicating, and doing.

Resiliency research provides us with a realistic reason to be hopeful for today's kids and should be used as a basis for dealing with at-risk kids rather than risk research, which offers a perspective of conditions that may contribute to the potency of their adverse experiences. Too often, prevention and intervention strategies developed from risk-focused research are value-laden. In contrast, resiliency-based programs are survivor focused. The obvious conclusion is that we need to focus our strategies *positively*. Instead of identifying risk, we can build programs that will enhance coping and other health-supported choices.

Traits of the Resilient Child

Characteristic	Noted by*
Had nondistressing habits during infancy	W
Is good natured; has affectionate disposition	R W
Has relationship with caring adult	R W G A
Communicates effectively	R G
Has sense of personal worthiness	R W G A
Has sense of control over "fate"	G A
Is effective in work, play, and love	G
Has positive social orientation; is cooperative	R W G A
Asks for help; is assertive	G A
Is above average in social intelligence	R G
Has informal support network	R W G A
Has ability to have close relationships	R G A
Has healthy expectations and needs	W G
Uses talents to personal advantage	R
Delays gratification	R W G A
Has internal locus of control	R W G A
Is flexible	R G
Has belief in his/her self-efficacy (belief system)	W G A
Has desire to improve	G
Has interpersonal sensitivity	R W
Has problem-solving ability	R W G A
Has decision-making ability	G A
Has future orientation	R W
Has trust and hope	G A
Exhibits and manages a range of emotions	G A
Possesses productive critical thinking skills	R W G A
Has a sense of humor	R G A

*R = Rutter   W = Werner   G = Garmezy   A = Anthony

Several years ago when I worked as a counselor, I usually found myself trying to alleviate problems—problems that too often couldn't be solved: alcoholism, generational poverty, violence in the neighborhood, emotional neglect. I often felt a sense of failure and found it easy to blame parents for everything bad in a child's life.

The resiliency research has helped me refocus. I now say, "What is working in your life?" instead of "What is wrong?" I try to convey to the kids that they have control of their lives by having the power to respond positively to the hand that life has dealt each of them. Jack Canfield offers a model for self-esteem: the formula $E + R = O$.[10] The *Event* (not in our control) plus the *Response* (in our control) equals the *Outcome* (what we live with).

Taking charge of perception and attitude, and then framing experiences in the positive, can literally change the lives of children. As a helper in schools, I now view my role with at-risk kids in terms of a positive intervention that can help them turn their situations around for the greatest personal benefit.

All kids, regardless of life circumstance, deserve the best chance possible to become successful. The activities in this book should serve as a means to make connections with kids and to effect that relationship of influence. But beyond the relationship and connection, these activities have the potential to engender skills, attitudes, and beliefs consistent with the resiliency research.

ADULTS MAKE A DIFFERENCE

Do kids really need adults? Do adults make a difference?

Yes, absolutely. Adults do make a difference! A kid's relationship with an adult often becomes the means of believing the world is a safe place, that an individual can affect destiny, and that the future will not be bleak. Positive kid-adult relationships are influential. That is why learning to engage kids actively is so important.

The bottom line is that we need each other. Emmy E. Werner and Ruth S. Smith have cautioned that we risk losing a generation if we don't attend *now* to the natural social bonds needed for survival.[11] I have taken this challenge to heart. The activities in this book, a changed attitude, and a sense of your own worth may help you risk reaching out to kids. It's worth it. The kids need you.

NOTES

1. L. Tobin, *What to Do with a Child Like This? Inside the Lives of Troubled Children* (Duluth, MN: Whole Person Associates, 1991), 9.

2. Albert Einstein, as quoted by Lynn Stoddard in *Redesigning Education: A Guide for Developing Human Greatness* (Tucson, AZ: Zephyr, 1992), 4.

3. Lynn Stoddard, *Redesigning Education*, 3.

4. A number of works by Michael Rutter are listed in the bibliography.

5. Julius Segal, *Winning Life's Toughest Battles: Roots of Human Resilience* (New York: Ballantine, 1987).

6. Norman Garmezy, foreword to *Vulnerable but Invincible: A Longitudinal Study of Resilient Children and Youth,* eds. Emmy E. Werner and Ruth S. Smith (New York: Adams, Bannister, and Cox, 1989).

7. The chart "Protective Factor Domains" is my synthesis and summary of research done by Norman Garmezy, Bonnie Benard, and Judy Falkenberg. The bibliography includes references to their works.

8. E. James Anthony and Bertram Cohler, eds., *The Invulnerable Child* (New York: Guilford, 1987).

9. See the bibliography for specific references to the works of Michael Rutter, Emmy E. Werner, Norman Garmezy, and E. James Anthony.

10. Jack Canfield, *Self-Esteem in the Classroom: A Self-Esteem Curriculum* (Pacific Palisades, CA: Self-Esteem Seminars, 1986).

11. Emmy E. Werner and Ruth S. Smith, *Vulnerable but Invincible: A Longitudinal Study of Resilient Children and Youth* (New York: Adams, Bannister, and Cox, 1989).

PART II

The Activities

THE CURRENT DEFINITION of literacy embraces a shift from the old paradigm of reading, writing, and arithmetic to employability, participatory citizenship, and the capacity to be effective in intimate relationships. The ability to communicate and interact positively will greatly influence future success.

No longer can we assume that the American dream is reachable. Today's youth must prepare for a world that we can't fathom. The current rate of change is so dramatic that even the futurists can only glimpse what might be. But if we can't totally prepare kids for their future, we can at least help them to become the best humans possible. Lynn Stoddard proposes a simple model that incorporates identity, interaction, and inquiry as the primary thrusts of a quality educational program.[1] I agree with Stoddard and embrace his model.

The challenge is clear. As caring adults in kids' lives, we must develop relationships that help to guide and foster positive attitudes that will contribute to future success. The words are far simpler than the effort they represent. We have to develop relationships that matter *to the kids*. We have to meet them where they are, in ways that make sense to them. Play, humor, and fun—some of the best springboards to trust and cooperation—will enhance the quality of any relationship. Stephen Covey prescribes trust and cooperation as the only means to win/win situations.[2] Anything less, and somebody loses.

My purpose in writing this book is to help kids win more, play more, and be more optimistic about their future. The activities in the next two chapters are designed to provide the kinds of experiences kids need to view themselves and their world in positive terms.

Age Appropriateness

Generally, the activities included here are appropriate for kids in fifth through twelfth grades. However, all the activities can be adapted for all kinds of kids in all kinds of situations. How can they have such broad utility? Simple. The impact is in the facilitation of the activity, not the content of the activity. The helper takes on the responsibility of matching the activity to the students. The activity becomes the window dressing for the goals of the group.

Guidelines based on chronological age are not very helpful, but I do attempt to choose themes that are consistent with the stage of development of the kids in my group. My personal age-appropriate themes are the following:

Ages 3–5: play, productivity, and touch

Ages 5–7: friendship and safety

Ages 7–10: helping, dealing with hurt feelings, and decisions about making friends

Ages 10–13: conflict, anger, loss, choices, and the future

Ages 13–16: coping, stress, anger, parents, and choosing healthy activities

Ages 16–25: hope, locus of control, future, sex, and emerging adulthood

For any of the above age groups, I will use the themes suggested plus all those preceding the given age range. And themes simply start the process. Match the activity to the theme, weave in some intention, and you've got a process.

Truly, the issue is not so much age appropriateness as it is relationship appropriateness. When considering the age, the helper uses standards that reflect typical age considerations. For example, safety is often an issue in age appropriateness: "Do not use this toy with children under the age of seven."

The problem with age standards is that too often they don't match children's real-life experiences. I challenge you to create your own barometer through a critical review of your relationship with the group you are serving. For example, if your group is comprised of kids who have no history with one another and no apparent similarities, your goal will be to bring them together through a common experience. You might begin by asking kids to tell the group what their names mean to them. Or you might ask them what name they would choose for their firstborn child. The dialogue between adults and kids is the goal, not the content of the discussion.

Group Cohesion

In addition to age appropriateness, the level of group cohesion is important. Make sure that your group of kids has the appropriate level of cohesion for the activity chosen.

Low cohesion:
The group members do not know one another's names. The group has met fewer than three times. Rules are evolving and the leader has not yet established influence.

Medium cohesion:
Rules and roles are easily discernible. Leader function is clear, observed, and respected. Norms are supportive of members, and the arena for disclosure is safety netted with clear understanding of confidentiality and positive feedback.

High cohesion:
The group functions with support from the leader but is independent of the leader role. Evidence of support is clear and members trust one another. Conflict is handled well.

The level of cohesion required is noted for each activity in this book. Most of the activities require low to medium cohesion. When in doubt, guess low. Never turn up the proverbial heat without a best guess of outcome. It is better to reinforce existing cohesion than it is to put kids in situations they are not prepared to handle.

Gauging Success

Choose activities from those provided here with a goal in mind. What do you want to create? You will know that an activity hits the mark within three to five minutes of giving the instructions. If the group is moving to accomplish the task or complete the activity assigned, then you have succeeded.

Pay attention to the group behavior. Don't try to second guess kids. You might even ask them, "Why do you suppose I have chosen this activity?" The participants give life to an activity by making it valid within the context of their experience. You set the stage, but the production is directed by the players in the game.

If the activity does not match the moment, the abilities, or the interests of the kids in your group, the kids will let you know. The group will lose focus and the noise level will become unbearable. If this occurs, tell the kids the truth—that you did not choose well. Don't blame the kids for the fact that the activity chosen did not serve your purpose.

Finally, it is important to have fun. Regardless of why you bought this book, all the activities here can provide new experiences for your special group of kids. Good luck!

NOTES

1. Lynn Stoddard, *Redesigning Education: A Guide for Developing Human Greatness* (Tucson, AZ: Zephyr, 1992).

2. Stephen R. Covey, *The Seven Habits of Highly Effective People* (New York: Simon & Schuster, 1989).

CHAPTER 4
Relating Activities

BEING ABLE TO MAKE CONNECTIONS WITH OTHERS is paramount to a quality life. I, for one, sought a career that allows me to contribute to the quality of the next generation. I believe that contributing to how kids make connections truly affects how they are able to relate to the world and how they contribute their own effectiveness and competence in the world. I can think of no more important subject for adults to teach, promote, and support.

The activities in this chapter are designed to help underscore the teaching points of effective communication and interaction. Most of the activities call for personal disclosure; some also create avenues for sharing ideas and experiences that acknowledge our complex society. Our children will be asked to interact in a multicultural world where consensus about how things "should be" no longer exists.

I cannot predict the future, but I do know that discussing, dialoguing, and sharing are the fodder for management of the new world order. We must teach our children to place a high value on the ability to use words, feelings, ideas, and wonderment to relate to others. I hope these activities help you make connections with the kids who are important to you.

Four Corners

Group Cohesion Low

Target Lessons Positive social orientation

Cooperation

Asking for help

Assertiveness

Team development

Developing an informal
support network

Materials Needed None

Space Requirement Large room with four distinct corners

For the Kids This activity focuses on how groups work together. Your job
is to participate to your utmost ability.

For the Facilitator

1. Ask participants to divide up equally into the four corners
   of the room.

2. Ask each group to do something, such as "Use your bodies to
   spell _____." Alternatively, ask each group to choose a
   "runner" to be in charge of collecting a certain number of items.

   For example:

   I need ten white athletic shoes tied together by the laces.

   I want three lipsticks and a fingernail file (junior high
   age and up).

3. The first group to finish is acknowledged. Another round
   is initiated.

Debrief How did you work together?

How was leadership established?

What did you notice about yourselves?

Hands

Group Cohesion   Low

Target Lessons   Personal worthiness

Self-evaluation

Use of individual talents to personal advantage

Materials Needed   Drawing paper

Pens or pencils

Scissors

For the Kids   Outline your hands on a piece of paper. On each digit describe something you do that deserves applause.

For the Facilitator

1. Talk about the need to feel good about yourself and the need to notice positive attributes. Discuss the value of feeling good. Define self-esteem as when you are safe, you feel competent, and you sense you are in control.

2. Discuss safety, competence, and control.

3. Allow time for each child to trace his/her hands and write a positive attribute inside the outline of each finger.

4. Divide children into random groups of six to eight kids each or allow three or four rounds of pairs.

5. Allow time for everyone to share the drawings with members of the group.

Debrief   What did you notice while doing this activity?

How did you feel about yourself?

What was this activity like for you?

Quilting

Group Cohesion   Low

Target Lessons   Reflective thinking
Critical thinking
Self-evaluation
Personal worthiness
Positive social orientation
Cooperation
Effective communication
Accepting cultural diversity

Materials Needed   Construction paper
Glue
Paints
Colored markers or crayons
Yarn
Pipe cleaners
Tape

For the Kids   Create a square for nine of the most important events in your life. Tape the squares together to make a quilt.

For the Facilitator   1. Talk with the group about quilts, including their historical significance.

2. Instruct each child to think about the significant events in his/her life and to pick nine events to depict on nine squares of paper.

3. Make the art supplies available. Give the kids plenty of time to prepare the quilt squares.

4. Divide kids into random groups of six to eight members.

5. Allow time for kids to share their quilts with others in the group.

Debrief   What did you learn? (Try to focus on how complex our lives are, yet how they are also simple.)

Copycats

Group Cohesion   Low

Target Lessons   Sense of humor
Interpersonal sensitivity

Materials Needed   None

For the Kids   Have you ever had a friend
who seemed just like you?
You thought and felt the
same way? You were in sync?

For the Facilitator

1. Have kids pair up and stand facing each other. Ask kids in each pair to identify themselves as either "A" or "B."

2. Ask the As to move *slowly* and *smoothly* while the Bs attempt to copy those movements. Encourage slow and smooth movements. The goal is to have the pairs successfully move in unison. (The goal is *not* to have one partner trick the other.)

3. After a few minutes, ask the Bs to lead while the As copy.

4. Conclude by having the partners move together without either one acting as the leader.

Debrief   What happens when you get in sync?

How does this feel?

How Many?

Group Cohesion   Low

Target Lessons   Interpersonal sensitivity

Positive social orientation

Cooperation

Materials Needed   None

For the Kids   We are all alike in some ways. Believe it? Or not?

For the Facilitator

1. Read aloud questions that begin with the words, "How many of you . . ."

   For example:

have been lonely?	have brothers and sisters?
have ever had a nightmare?	have fights with your mother?
have ever won an award?	have taken candy from a store?
like to eat tacos?	fart and blame it on others?

   Prepare your questions to focus on the subject you want to highlight.

2. Instruct kids who have had the experience or who agree with the statement to raise their hands.

3. Ask kids wishing to comment on the topic to raise their hands.

Restrictions/Cautions   This activity is intended to promote inclusion! Your questions should be "safe" to ensure that the kids will experience success.

Debrief   What happens to a group when group members notice similarities?

How can we use this phenomenon at school?

Ta-Too-Ta-Ta

Group Cohesion   Low

Target Lessons   Sense of humor
Tolerance

Materials Needed   None

Space Requirement   Large activity area

For the Kids   You are going to follow everything I do, say everything I say,
and then sing a chorus of "Ta-Too-Ta-Ta" together.

For the Facilitator
1. Explain that you want the kids to imitate your gestures and
   actions as well as repeat your words. For example, say "Thumbs
   up" and demonstrate thumbs up. Ask them to put their thumbs
   up and say "Thumbs up."

2. Sing a chorus of "Ta-Too-Ta-Ta" three times in an exaggerated
   manner, then ask the kids to sing it with you.

3. Repeat this process, adding movements and their verbal
   descriptions in a sequence until you have a rhythm going.
   For example: Thumbs up (kids repeat and do), elbows together
   (kids repeat and do), knees together (kids repeat and do), buns
   out (kids repeat and do)—then all together: "Ta-Too-Ta-Ta,
   Ta-Too-Ta-Ta, Ta-Too-Ta-Ta." Continue until they run out of
   steam (or you do).

Debrief   Did you get confused?

Did you get better?

Was doing this easier the more you did it? Why?

Find Me

Group Cohesion   Low

Target Lessons   Positive social orientation

Cooperation

Asking for help

Assertiveness

Team development

Developing an informal support network

Materials Needed   3 × 5–inch index cards with several physical traits listed

Pens or pencils

For the Kids   It's a scavenger hunt! Find one person for each physical characteristic listed on the index card. Write that person's name next to the description on the card—each name only one time. When you have filled out the card completely, you can sit down.

For the Facilitator   1. Give each child a 3 × 5 card listing physical traits of those in the room. (For example: brown eyes, blond hair, eyeglasses, tall, short.)

2. Tell the kids that this activity is like a scavenger hunt; they must find another kid in the room to match each of the traits listed, then write that kid's name next to the appropriate trait. Tell the kids that they can write their own names next to only one trait, they can use only one name per trait, and they cannot use any name more than once. Say "Go!"

3. After five minutes or so, have all the kids return to their seats. Call out a trait and have all the kids who have that trait stand.

4. Have kids notice the traits that have lots of people standing and those that don't.

Variations Change the framework of the scavenger hunt to incorporate different information.

For example:

Who knows how to play the piano?

Who knows how to swim?

Who lives in an apartment?

Who has two brothers?

Who knows the definition of . . .?

Who can solve the following problem . . .?

Who can draw an example of . . .?

Who can demonstrate . . .?

Debrief Was it hard to get the names?

Were your expectations met?

Were there any surprises?

What is the lesson here?

Do You Love Your Neighbor?

Group Cohesion   Low

Target Lessons   Sense of humor
Positive social orientation
Cooperation

Materials Needed   None

Space Requirement   Large activity area or gym

For the Kids   Get into a large circle and connect with those on both sides of you by holding hands.

For the Facilitator
1. Explain: When I yell, "1-2-3," you yell back, "Do you love your neighbor?" Then I yell (for example), "Yes! Especially if you are wearing tennis shoes." Next, everyone wearing tennis shoes has to run to a new place in the circle that's at least ten spaces away. While the people who are wearing tennis shoes are running around the circle looking for a new place, the people who aren't wearing tennis shoes are trying to close up the circle by joining hands, trying to trap the runners in the middle.

2. Continue to call out different characteristics until the kids run out of steam. Use characteristics that are fun and good humored—no put-downs. You can use feelings, traits, or situations.

   For example:

blonde hair	ever got an A
brushed teeth this morning	wears glasses
likes someone else in the room	has ever been lonely
has argued with parents	has ever lost a friend

Restrictions/Cautions   Play safely. You may have to modify this activity for people with special needs or limited mobility.

Debrief   Were there any surprises?

Why did we play this?

What purpose does the game have?

Elephants and Giraffes

Group Cohesion Low

Target Lessons Sense of humor
Effective communication

Materials Needed None

For the Kids Everyone get into a big circle. Think about elephants and giraffes. How do they look?

For the Facilitator

1. Have everyone get into a big circle.

2. Pick someone to be "it" in the middle.

3. "It" walks around the circle and all of a sudden points to someone and says either "elephant!" or "giraffe!"

4. The person pointed to is "picked." The picked kid *plus* the two kids on either side of him/her have to the count of three to assume a pose imitating the animal called.

   For example:

   Elephant: The picked kid holds one arm out like a trunk. The two kids on either side hold their hands up to the middle person's head like two big ears.

   Giraffe: The picked kid stretches his/her neck up and out. The kids on either side hold their arms up to form circles near the middle person's sides to represent spots.

   If the three fail to form the correct positions within the given time, the middle person becomes "it."

5. Go several rounds.

Variations You can make up gestures to represent any animal.

Debrief What makes this activity funny?

What did it feel to act like an animal?

What happened to the group after the activity?

On One Hand
and on the Other Hand

Group Cohesion Low

Target Lessons Personal worthiness
Exhibiting and managing a range of emotions
Belief in one's self-efficacy

Materials Needed Paper plates
Colored markers or crayons

For the Kids We are all complex. Everyone has different feelings and experiences. What about you is unique or different?

For the Facilitator 1. Have the kids trace their left hands on one side of a paper plate and number the fingers from one to five.

2. Have them write the answers to five questions, one answer on each finger.

For example:

What kind of music do you like?

What kind of sports do you play (or like or dislike)?

What pets do you have (or wish you had)?

What was your favorite vacation?

What do you dislike (or like) about school?

Vary the questions depending on the material, information, or feelings you want to elicit. These answers represent who kids are on the outside, "on one hand."

3. On the other side of the paper plate, have the kids trace their right hands and ask riskier questions, again varied depending on the answers/feelings you want to elicit.

   For example:

   What makes you mad (or sad)?

   If you could change one thing about your life, what would it be?

   What do you wish you did well?

   Where do you see yourself in five years?

   Where do you see yourself as an adult?

   These questions represent kids' inner feelings, "on the other hand."

4. Put kids in pairs or small groups so they can share their responses with one another.

Debrief What happened when you completed the assignment?

How did it feel to share with someone else?

Building Blocks

Group Cohesion   Low

Target Lessons   Critical thinking

Data analysis

Self-evaluation

Effective communication

Friendship

Materials Needed   Worksheet 1 (prepared before the activity)

Tape

Colored markers or crayons

Scissors

For the Kids   Prepare a set of "building blocks" to answer these kinds of questions: "What helps you when you're in a crisis?" "What contributes to your happiness?" "How do you solve a problem?"

For the Facilitator
1. Articulate the need for foundations in building life-style skills and attitudes. Provide links in the metaphor of building a skyscraper and building a life.

2. Discuss values, mores, beliefs, and hopes as part of everyone's life foundation.

3. Give each group member several copies of Worksheet 1. Allow kids plenty of time to cut out and prepare blocks representing the foundation securing their lives.

4. Allow time for everyone to share his/her blocks, either in small groups or in pairs.

Debrief   What was the purpose of this activity?

Why is a foundation such a big deal?

Why do people need to think about their lives?

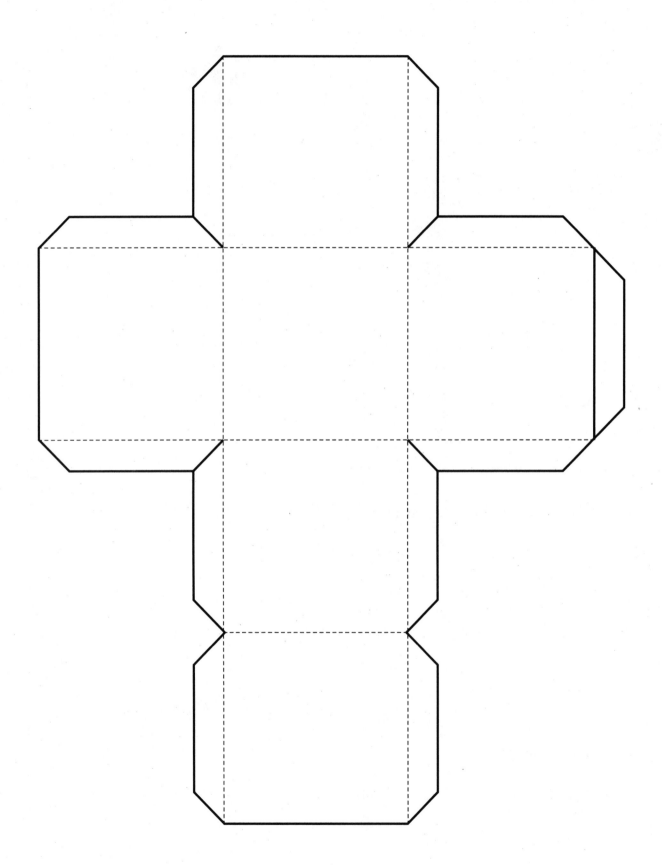

Human Bingo

Group Cohesion   Low

Target Lessons   Positive social orientation

Cooperation

Developing an informal support network

Materials Needed   Worksheet 2 (prepared before the activity)

Pens or pencils

For the Kids   We are going to play bingo!

For the Facilitator

1. Pass out bingo cards (Worksheet 2) with characteristics already on them.

   For example:

   got an A on an English test last week

   looks up numbers in the phone book instead of dialing directory assistance

   likes *all* his/her teachers

   has a niece or nephew

   has recently helped a friend with homework

   is left-handed

   favorite TV program is a detective show

   has more than one sibling

   likes to draw cartoons

2. Explain the rules:

   Find one person who fits the description in each square.

   When you've found someone, ask the person to sign his or her full name in the appropriate square.

   Each name can be used only one time.

   When you have a name in each square, yell "bingo!"

Debrief   What did you learn?

Why is this important?

HUMAN BINGO...

Pepper, Where's My Pepper?

Group Cohesion   Low

Target Lessons   Interpersonal sensitivity

Accepting cultural diversity

Developing an informal
support network

Materials Needed   A tray with about 25 green peppers (the skinny kind
with the little caps work best)

For the Kids   Think about peppers. How would you describe them?

For the Facilitator

1. Separate the kids into groups of eight to ten members.

2. Place the peppers on a tray so they can be seen by the whole
   group.

3. Ask the kids to describe the characteristics of the peppers. Have
   them shout out the characteristics.

   For example:

   They're green!   They're oblong!

   They have stems!   They're shiny!

4. Have each group pick a leader. Ask the leaders of each group to
   come up and pick one pepper, choosing carefully. Have the
   leaders return to their groups with their chosen peppers.

5. Have each group examine the pepper they have. Ask the kids to
   think about what makes it unique, what distinguishes it from
   the rest. They can smell the pepper, roll it, give it a name, measure it—but warn them that they cannot eat or mark the pepper.

6. Ask the leaders to return their peppers to the tray.

7. Ask the groups, one at a time, to describe their peppers. While
   they are doing that, mix up the peppers on the tray.

8. Ask the leaders to return to the tray to find their original
   peppers, then return to their groups.

Debrief   Could you find your pepper?

Do you feel different about the peppers on the tray
now that you "know" one?

What did you learn? Why is this important?

Button, Button

Group Cohesion	Low
Target Lessons	Effective communication
	Effectiveness in work, play, and love
	Interpersonal sensitivity
	Exhibiting and managing a range of emotions
	Developing an informal support network
	Cooperation
Materials Needed	Colored paper (cut into large "button" shapes)
	Colored markers or crayons
	Safety or straight pins
For the Kids	Celebrate your personal gifts! What are they? What did special people give you? Decorate your buttons with remarkable gifts of support from others.
For the Facilitator	1. Have each child design his or her own personal buttons and put them on with the safety or straight pins.
	2. Divide kids into random groups of six to eight members. Have them talk with one another about their buttons, or have them interview one another in three or four rounds of pairs.
Variations	Vary the questions according to the material, information, and feelings you want to elicit.
Debrief	How was it to make your buttons?
	Did you have any fantasies?

Who Am I?

Group Cohesion   Low

Target Lessons   Fairness
Effective communication
Data analysis

Materials Needed   3 × 5–inch index cards
Masking tape

For the Kids   How would you give clues to identify yourself? Who are we anyway?

For the Facilitator

1. Line up kids in two rows, back to back.

2. Hand each person a 3 × 5 card with the name of someone else in the group on it and a small piece of masking tape.

3. Have each person in the first row use the masking tape to attach the card to the back of the person in the second row. Reverse the procedure so every kid has a card taped to his/her back.

4. Each person walks around the room asking questions about the person whose name appears on the card on his/her back. The questions can be answered only yes or no.

   For example:

   Am I a male?

   Am I wearing green?

   Does my name begin with an "M"?

5. After kids guess the names on their cards, they can take the cards off and sit down with the others who have also guessed correctly.

6. Allow enough time for most or all of the kids to guess their mystery names.

Variations   Use different mystery subjects for the cards—for example, the names of cartoon characters, animals, or historical figures.

Debrief   How difficult was the task?

What helped you figure out your name?

Crazy Eights

Group Cohesion   Low

Target Lessons   Global perspective
Tolerance
Data analysis
Reflective thinking

Materials Needed   Drawing paper (two pieces for each pair)
Colored markers or crayons

For the Kids   We are going to focus on how alike *and* how different we all are.

For the Facilitator   1. Pair participants.

2. Have the kids identify eight ways they are alike.

3. Have the kids identify eight ways they are different.

4. Have them draw two pictures: one illustrating their similarities and one illustrating their differences.

Restrictions/Cautions   Don't pair friends.

Debrief   What did you find out about your partner? Anything interesting?

What did you find out about yourself?

Which was easier, identifying differences or similarities?

Do you feel you know your partner better as a result of this activity?

How about yourself?

Personal Trivia

Group Cohesion   Low

Target Lessons   Data analysis

Interpersonal sensitivity

Personal worthiness

Exhibiting and managing a range of emotions

Materials Needed   Paper or paper plates

Pens or pencils

For the Kids   We are going to play a trivia game about ourselves!

For the Facilitator

1. Each kid takes a piece of paper or a paper plate and on the front writes the numbers 1 through 4.

2. Make up and announce descriptions for the four categories.

   For example:

   1 = hobby

   2 = family

   3 = vacation

   4 = school

3. Have the kids write on the paper or plate a question that applies to themselves for each category.

   For example:

   1 = Who plays the harp?

   2 = Who has two brothers, two sisters, two stepbrothers, and two stepsisters?

   3 = Who went to Europe alone during sophomore year?

   4 = Who has never had a detention?

4. Have the kids form small groups. Have them shuffle the papers or plates, then exchange them.

5. Each kid takes a turn reading the questions on the new paper or plate. The group has to guess who is being described.

Variations If the group seems reticent, continue self-disclosure and have the kids answer questions within their small groups.

For example:

What makes me mad?

What is my favorite possession?

What is my most meaningful experience?

If I could change anything about my life, what would I change?

What makes me sad?

What do I do well?

When was the last time I felt successful or proud of myself?

What is a dream that I want to come true for myself
or for the world?

Debrief What did you learn?

How did you handle the task?

How did it feel to disclose personal information?

Silent Line-Ups

Group Cohesion   Low

Target Lessons   Sense of humor
Effective communication

Materials Needed   None

Space Requirement   A room big enough for a line or circle of those present

For the Kids   We have to do this without talking. Everything I ask you to do has to be done silently!

For the Facilitator   Tell the kids they have to line up without verbal communication in order of (for example) their birthdate, their height, the size of their feet, the size of their hands, or the length of their hair. This is a good way to separate friends and line up folks to be counted off into random small groups.

Debrief   What were the easiest methods of organization?

What did you learn?

Touch

Group Cohesion   Low-Medium

Target Lessons   Positive social orientation
Cooperation
Trust and hope
Flexibility

Materials Needed   None

Space Requirement   Large activity area

For the Kids   Everybody stand up. I will call out a description of someone. You will have to find the person who has that characteristic and *touch* him or her.

For the Facilitator
1. Explain that the object of the game is to find and then touch the person who has the characteristic you describe.

2. Explain that touching has to be appropriate: no roughhousing and no touching "sacred places." When kids find and touch the person described, they keep touching him/her until the next characteristic is called out.

3. Call out characteristics, allowing enough time between calls for *all* the kids to find someone to touch. (For example: Touch someone who is wearing blue . . . has glasses on . . . is over 14.)

4. Depending on the group and your focus, you can move to more complex characteristics. (For example: Touch someone who you know has been lonely . . . whose parents are divorced.)

Note   This is a great activity to help include outsiders. For example, if a student in a wheelchair is wearing pink, I'll say, "Touch someone who is wearing pink."

Debrief   Was this game fun?

Was it hard to touch someone at first?

What made it easier?

What did you learn?

Picnic Basket

Group Cohesion Low-Medium

Target Lessons Future orientation

Gratitude

Reflective thinking

Desire to improve

Self-evaluation

Developing an informal support network

Materials Needed Small pieces of paper or 3 × 5–inch index cards

Construction paper

Colored markers or crayons

Scissors

Tape

For the Kids We are all given a picnic basket when we are born. Parents are supposed to fill the basket until the child is independent. Then the child cares for his or her own basket.

What do you bring to the picnic?

What are all the things that make you uniquely you?

What do you need for a full picnic?

For the Facilitator 1. Read the story above to the kids and ask the questions.

2. Have each person make a picnic basket out of construction paper.

3. Have the kids write positive and negative life experiences on slips of paper or 3 × 5 cards (this is the "picnic"). Have them place the papers or cards into their own baskets.

4. Allow the kids time to prepare their baskets and their picnic of experiences—good and bad.

5. Divide kids into random groups of six to eight members. Each small group allows for individual sharing.

6. Each group then discusses the similarities and differences among group members and their picnic baskets.

Debrief Do you believe that life is like a picnic?

Do you have a full basket?

What happened for you during this activity?

Dressing Up

Group Cohesion   Low-Medium

Target Lessons   Problem solving

Reflective thinking

Effective communication

Using individual talents to personal advantage

Materials Needed   Strips of paper

Colored markers or crayons

Masking tape

For the Kids   Think about the people here and the special or wonderful things you know about each other. We're going to get all dressed up!

For the Facilitator
1. Have the kids form groups of four to eight members.

2. Pass out strips of paper, markers or crayons, and a roll of masking tape to each group. There should be enough strips of paper so that each person can write on two strips for every kid in his/her group. (For example, if the groups each have four kids, then each person in each group should have eight strips of paper.)

3. Have the kids write two positive statements—things they think are special or that they like about each kid in their group. Emphasize that there should be no put-downs or teasing. Allow them time to think and write.

   For example:

   I really like your sense of humor.   You have a nice voice.

   You have beautiful hair.   You are a good friend.

   I'm glad I know you.

4. After the kids have finished writing on the slips of paper, they get to stick the slips onto the other kids in their group with pieces of masking tape. Caution them to stick the strips only on appropriate places. No roughhousing.

Debrief   How does it feel to be "all dressed up"?

Was it hard to think of nice things to write about other people?

How did you feel after you read your messages?

Were you surprised at what people wrote about you?

Why is this lesson important?

What's Different?

Group Cohesion Low-Medium

Target Lessons Effective communication
Positive social orientation
Cooperation
Developing an informal
support network

Materials Needed None

For the Kids Are you good at noticing? Would you be a good witness to a crime? Let's check.

For the Facilitator 1. Have everyone pair up and face each other.

2. Have kids in each pair decide who is "A" and who is "B" by using some measurement (for example, A has the smallest feet).

3. Ask As in each pair to memorize everything they notice or see about Bs. Allow 20 seconds.

4. Then ask the pairs to turn back-to-back so the Bs will have time to change something about themselves. (Examples of changes: a watch turned upside down, a sock rolled down, a barrette put in a different way.)

5. Have pairs turn around and face each other again. Ask As to guess what Bs have changed.

6. Have the kids switch roles so the Bs can guess what the As have changed.

Variations You can start off with one change and go up to as many as seems fun and accomplishable for each particular group.

Restrictions/Cautions At first, some kids won't sit face to face or may be uncomfortable with the close scrutiny involved in this exercise. This discomfort usually disappears after the first round. Avoid requests for too many changes—this could inhibit creativity.

Debrief Why is observation so important?

What did you learn about yourself?

What did you learn about your partner?

My Square

Group Cohesion Low-Medium

Target Lessons Effective communication
Problem solving
Data analysis

Materials Needed Construction paper
Pens or pencils
Scissors

For the Kids We are putting the pieces of our lives together. What are your special pieces?

For the Facilitator

1. Pass out the paper, pens or pencils, and scissors. Have the kids cut a square of paper into at least eight pieces.

2. Ask the kids, "If you were cut into eight pieces, how would they be titled?"

3. Ask the kids to write a few words on each piece of paper to reflect something important in their lives. (For example: brothers, sisters, teachers, family, friends, principal, dreams, wishes/hopes, heroes/heroines.)

4. Allow them time to share their squares with others, either in pairs or in small groups.

Variations You can cut the squares ahead of time if time or scissor use is a factor.

Debrief Why did you pick those eight pieces?

What would you change?

Thank-You Notes

Group Cohesion   Low-Medium

Target Lessons   Effective communication
Reflective thinking
Using individual talents to personal advantage
Problem solving

Materials Needed   Ready-made note cards or note paper
Colored markers or crayons

For the Kids   We are going to write thank-you notes!

For the Facilitator

1. Have the kids form groups of four to six members.

2. Talk with kids about the importance of expressing appreciation as well as the joy of receiving those expressions.

3. Have them write thank-you notes to one another, one note for each member of their group. They can decorate them if they like. Give some examples of what they might write:

   Thanks for being my friend.

   I'm glad you are in my group—thanks for being here.

   Thank you for sharing your . . .

4. Allow plenty of time for the note writing.

5. Let the kids exchange their notes.

Debrief   How did you feel when you had to write the notes?

How did you feel when you received a thank-you note?

What did you learn?

Balloons and Anchors

Group Cohesion Medium

Target Lessons Positive social orientation
Cooperation
Flexibility
Self-evaluation

Materials Needed Worksheet 3 (prepared before the activity) or construction paper
Pens or pencils
Yarn
Scissors
Glue

For the Kids What brings you up? What pulls you down?

For the Facilitator
1. Make enough copies of Worksheet 3 so each kid will have one. If the kids are older, they can draw the balloon and the anchor themselves.

2. Discuss: Each of us experiences periods of good times and periods of bad times. Give examples. Do bad things ever become good? Do good things ever become bad?

3. Ask the kids to think about their "ups" and "downs." Have them decorate the balloons to represent the ups and the anchors to represent the downs.

4. Break the group into pairs. Allow three minutes for each individual to share with his/her partner.

5. Change partners two to four times or use small groups of six to eight children.

6. Talk with the entire group about similarities and differences in their ups and downs.

Debrief Were there any surprises?

What did you notice?

How did you like the activity?

My Many Faces

Group Cohesion Medium

Target Lessons Exhibiting and managing a range of emotions

Developing an informal support network

Personal worthiness

Materials Needed Worksheet 4 (prepared before the activity) or drawing paper

Colored markers or crayons

For the Kids Emotions make the world go around. All emotions come from these three basic ones: sad, mad, and glad. We are going to do an inventory of all the emotions.

For the Facilitator 1. Make enough copies of Worksheet 4 so each kid has one. Older kids can draw their own sad, mad, and glad faces.

2. Ask the kids to draw other "emotional" faces that reflect how they feel at other times. (For example: worried, anxious, confused, terrified, disappointed, hurt, lonely, betrayed, scared, overwhelmed, excited, grateful.)

3. Ask the kids to identify what is happening when they are experiencing these feelings. Have them write under each feeling face a description of a situation that elicits each emotion.

4. Conduct one-to-one interviews with student pairs. Are there similarities in experiences? In feelings?

Debrief Why are emotions so hard to talk about?

How many emotions are there?

Friendship Want Ads

Group Cohesion   Medium

Target Lessons   Cooperation

Assertiveness

Asking for help

Positive social orientation

Effectiveness in work, play, and love

Materials Needed   Paper

Pens or pencils

Tape

For the Kids   We are going to look through the want ads, but we have to write them first!

For the Facilitator   1. Provide an example of a want ad. Pass out the paper, pens or pencils, and tape.

2. Ask the kids to write a "friend wanted" ad describing characteristics they look for in a friend. (You may want to assign the kids numbers or fictitious names so when they read one another's ads, they won't know who belongs to each ad.)

3. Ask the kids to write a "friend offered" ad describing qualities they bring to a friendship.

4. Post their ads. Ask kids to pick one "friend wanted" and one "friend offered." They can't pick their own. (This part is more revealing if they have used numbers or fictitious names.)

5. Kids interview one another as they answer "want ads."

Debrief   What did you find out about one another?

What did you find out about yourself?

Why is it important to ask for what you want?

Red Light, Yellow Light, Green Light

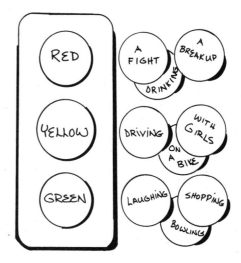

Group Cohesion Medium

Target Lessons Positive social orientation
Cooperation
Self-evaluation
Personal worthiness
Interpersonal sensitivity
Problem solving
Decision making
Critical thinking
Close personal relationships, friendships

Materials Needed Worksheet 5 (prepared before the activity) or drawing paper

Colored markers or crayons

For the Kids *Red light:* What have you done that you wished you had stopped? What stops you now?

Yellow light: When should you be cautious? How have you learned to be cautious?

Green light: What have you just gone ahead and done without hesitation?

For the Facilitator 1. Talk about the varied stop light meanings:

   Red for situations you wish you could have controlled.

   Yellow for situations that have been hazardous.

   Green for situations that have been healthy and growth inducing.

2. Instruct each person to prepare a creative response to "What are *your* red, yellow, and green lights?" Give each one a copy of Worksheet 5, or have older kids make their own. The worksheet allows each kid to think of and write in the appropriate circle three red light situations, three yellow light situations, and three green light situations.

3. Provide time (about five minutes) for kids to interview one another in pairs.

4. Call "Pick a partner" and then "Now discuss *red* lights."
   Call "Pick a partner" and then "Now discuss *yellow* lights."
   Call "Pick a partner" and then "Now discuss *green* lights."
   Continue for four to six rounds.

Debrief   What is this new activity?

What have you thinking about your life in stoplight terms?

What happened for you?

What have you learned from your "lights"?

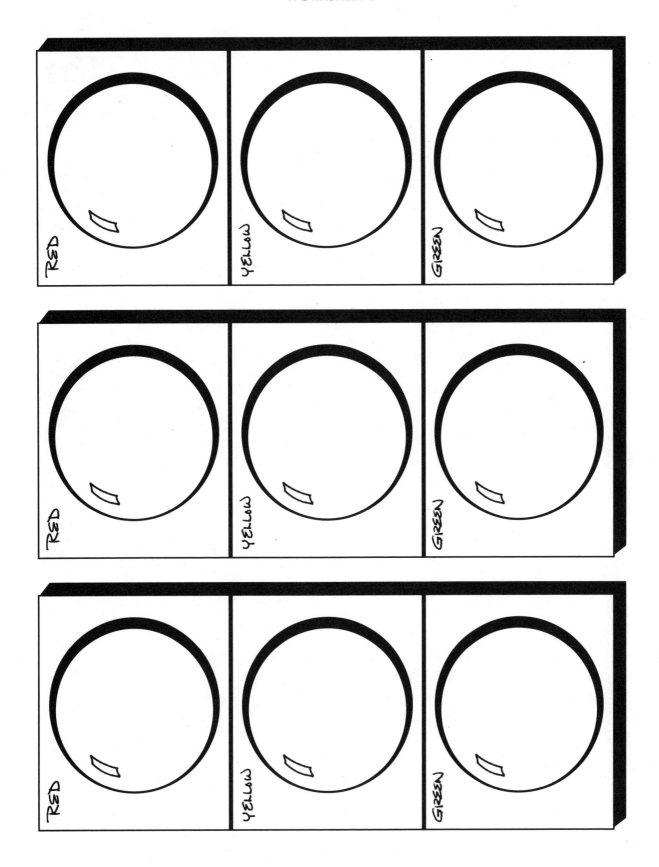

Life Map

Group Cohesion   Medium-High

Target Lessons   Effective communication
Reflective thinking
Global perspective
Positive social orientation
Cooperation
Interpersonal sensitivity
Healthy expectations and needs
Exhibiting and managing a range of emotions

Materials Needed   Drawing paper
Colored markers or crayons

For the Kids   What has changed in you? What has happened to you along life's path? What would you do differently? Who are the people that have helped or hindered?

For the Facilitator
1. Tell a brief story about yourself or someone else. Try to delineate the many life stages experienced.

2. Have the kids form pairs. Each child gets to talk about himself/herself for two minutes. After time is up, ask, "Is it difficult to talk about yourself?"

3. Instruct each child to create a map of his/her own life.

4. Have the kids share their maps in small groups or pairs.

Debrief   What kind of map will represent your future?

Who's in charge?

Were there any surprises?

What were the similarities and differences among the maps in your group?

Insides-Outsides

Group Cohesion Medium-High

Target Lessons Exhibiting and managing
a full range of emotions
Tolerance
Critical thinking
Reflective thinking
Stress management

Materials Needed Manila file folders
Colored markers or crayons

For the Kids *Outsides:* What do you let people see? What do you let
them know? Why?

Insides: What do you keep from others? What don't people
know about you? Why?

For the Facilitator
1. Discuss the difference between the public and private aspects
   of all individuals.

2. Give examples. (Public: daughter, Irish, born in Chicago,
   three siblings. Private: kid of alcoholic, mother left home,
   uncle has AIDS.)

3. Give each kid a manila file folder.

4. Ask the kids to decorate the outside of the folder to depict
   their public side and to decorate the inside of the folder to
   show their private side.

5. Provide an arena to share one to one or in small groups. Kids
   may share the insides of their folders at their discretion (never
   force them to disclose private information).

Variations See "On One Hand and on the Other Hand" on page 91 for
a more structured version of sharing that is more suitable for
younger children.

Debrief What are the similarities in your experiences?

Why is this lesson important?

Past, Present, Future

Group Cohesion   Medium-High

Target Lessons   Trust and hope

Future orientation

Personal worthiness

Self-evaluation

Problem solving

Decision making

Global perspective

Effective communication

Effectiveness in work, play, and love

Materials Needed   Drawing paper

Colored markers or crayons

For the Kids   What are your strongest memories from the past? From the present? What do you hope for the future?

For the Facilitator   1. Discuss life cycles: infancy, childhood, adolescence, and so on.

2. Ask each child to think of the past, the present, and the future, and then to creatively present his/her story using the art materials.

3. Pair the kids to start a disclosure process. Ask them, "How hard was this to do?"

4. Now create small groups. Let kids share histories and plans for the future.

5. Have each group look for similarities among their life cycles.

6. Have children report their noted similarities in the large group. Ask for volunteers to share those similarities that they didn't expect and those that are not surprises.

Debrief   Do people who don't look alike share experiences or dreams for the future?

What is your evidence of the similarities?

Board of Directors

Group Cohesion   Medium-High

Target Lessons   Self-evaluation
Future orientation
Personal worthiness
Effective communication
Critical thinking
Reflective thinking

Materials Needed   Drawing paper
Colored markers or crayons

For the Kids   Think about the people who have influenced you. What have they done to become a part of your life? How have they influenced you? Do they actively participate in your life? Do you want them there? Who sits at your "table" (explain that the table is a metaphor for sphere of influence)?

For the Facilitator
1. Explain the role of the CEO in a business. Explain the role of the Board of Directors.

2. Tell the kids that they are all CEOs for the day and that they are each going to have a "board meeting."

3. Explain "influence" (the power to get people to "do").

4. Ask the kids to think about who has influenced their lives. Have each person draw a "boardroom table" and the people of influence seated there.

5. Using pairs or small groups, have each kid introduce and describe his/her Board of Directors to the other kids in the group.

Variations   Create symbols to define the *kind* of relationships you have with the individuals at your table. Are these positive, nurturing relationships? Or relationships with conflict? Or both?

Debrief   What feelings did you have about your Board of Directors?

Are *you* influential in somebody else's life? Are you at someone else's boardroom table? What boards will you be on when you grow up?

Zipper Tag

Group Cohesion   Medium-High

Target Lessons   Effective communication

Fairness

Interpersonal sensitivity

Effectiveness in work, play, and love

Problem solving

Decision making

Critical thinking

Materials Needed   None

Space Requirement   Large activity area or gym

For the Kids   Find a partner—we are going to play Zipper Tag!

For the Facilitator

1. Explain: The game is Zipper Tag. You will pretend that everyone has a zipper running up and down his or her back. When your zipper is up, you can run around and unzip other people. When your zipper is down, you have to stay where you are and bend down, as if you have no energy.

   Now find a partner to zip up. Say "zip" when you do it. Have your partner zip you up. Now you are both "energized." These are the rules:

   When you are zipped up, you can go around and try to unzip other people—unless someone unzips you.

   When you are unzipped, you have to stop and bend over. Only your partner can zip you back up.

If both you and your partner get unzipped, you're dead in the water.

The object of the game is to stay zipped up and moving while trying to unzip everybody else. This is a game of strategy, a survival game. You must work to stay alive, and the only way to guarantee staying alive is by *not* killing. (I use this game a lot to teach about gangs. After the fifth or sixth time, kids realize that the only way for everybody to stay alive is for all kids to refrain from unzipping.)

2. Do this in rounds. In round one, two kids are partners. In round two, four kids are partners. In round three, eight kids are partners.

Variations   For Reverse Zipper Tag, begin in large teams of eight, then divide to teams of four, and finally divide into teams of two.

Restrictions/Cautions   This is a great warm-up/ice breaker and can also be used to blow off steam and have fun. Be sure kids play safely and make sure touching is appropriate and acceptable. Kids with limited mobility will need special help to play.

Debrief   What is the difference between having two and eight partners?

What did you learn about yourself? About your partners?

CHAPTER 5

Thinking Activities

I DON'T THINK I EVER THOUGHT ABOUT THINKING prior to college. I am not even sure if thinking was part of the college curriculum. I am sure that now I think about thinking as a part of my daily experience. I am mildly obsessed with coming up with ideas to initiate the critical thinking process in kids.

Recently, in a third-grade class I encountered a boy who was very noticeable and likeable. I enjoyed working with him. On my third visit to his classroom, he met me in the hall and said, "Oh, Michelle—today will be a thinking day." I laughed and said to him, "But every day should be a thinking day!" He paused, put his hand to the side of his face, and said, "I didn't know that!" I have since wondered how many other kids haven't grasped that education should be the provocation of original thought, not the regurgitation of someone else's thoughts.

I have come to believe that thinking can become a critical aspect of any kind of interaction. When applicability is pondered, you are thinking. When you relate one fact to another, it is thinking. When you discriminate in making a choice, thinking has occurred. Thinking can happen anywhere and everywhere.

Historically, thinking has not been a critical element of the educational process. Reproducing information, not producing it, has been central to how students are taught and judged: What they know is more important than what they can do with what they know. The shift from reproducing to producing is one of the most important aspects of the educational forecast for the future.

You can be ahead of the game by using activities like the ones here. Each activity attempts to provide an experience that can be generalized to real-life situations. Like the skills associated with relating, thinking—critically, creatively, and reflectively—enhances the potential for balancing stress with concrete coping. Together the relating and thinking skills create a repertoire of problem-solving strategies that may well reduce the risk of any adversity. Good luck!

Pretzels and Knots

Group Cohesion Low

Target Lessons Problem solving
Safety
Flexibility
Developing an informal
support network

Materials Needed None

For the Kids We are able to take control. There are always solutions
to our problems.

For the Facilitator
1. Form the group into one large circle or smaller circles
   of six to twelve people (must be an even number).

2. Ask kids to follow these instructions:

   Each person, raise your right hand.

   Now grab the right hand of a person in your circle who
   is *not* standing on either side of you.

   Now raise your left hand and grab hold of the left hand of
   someone in your circle. Remember, you cannot grab the
   hand of the person on either side of you.

   Okay, now you must untangle this knot you just created,
   but you cannot let go of the hands you are holding. Be careful
   not to hurt anyone!

   This can be done one, two, or three times, depending on how
   well the kids get untangled. Repeat the process until all groups
   have been successful. If a group is unable to get untangled, allow
   them to start again and work until they succeed.

Note There are three possible "answers" for this game: one large circle,
a figure eight, and two separate circles.

Restrictions/Cautions People with limited vision or mobility may need adjustments
to play this game.

Debrief How easy was this activity? How difficult?

What helped you untangle?

How does this activity apply to life?

Puzzler

Group Cohesion   Low

Target Lessons   Effective communication

Positive social orientation

Cooperation

Materials Needed   Postcards, magazine covers, or posters

Colored markers or crayons

Scissors

Envelopes

For the Kids   We're all pieces in a giant puzzle!

For the Facilitator

1. Before the activity, take several large postcards, magazine covers, or posters. Color the back of each one a different color. Cut into puzzle pieces and put each puzzle into an envelope.

2. Distribute the pieces to the kids, giving each kid one puzzle piece.

3. Instruct the kids to take their own puzzle pieces and go off to find the other pieces that go together to make up their puzzle. Kids must work in silence!

4. Once kids find the others who have pieces of their puzzle, they stay with that group.

Debrief   What happened when you tried to find the other puzzle pieces?

How did the process work?

What would have been different if speaking had been allowed?

Castles

Group Cohesion   Low

Target Lessons   Trust and hope

Healthy expectations and needs

Using individual talents to personal advantage

Problem solving

Cooperation

Materials Needed   Tons of 3 × 5–inch index cards (in colors, if possible)

For the Kids   Building a community is within reach! We can do what no one has done before . . . silently.

For the Facilitator
1. Get kids into small groups throughout the room.

2. Each group will create a structure from 3 × 5 cards. Older kids can easily use 500 cards per group; younger kids will only need 100 to 200 per group. The more cards the kids have and the more time, the more elaborate the structures will become. Explain the rules:

   You can fold the cards once, across the middle lengthwise (model it).

   You may not stack them flat, one on top of another.

   You *must* connect your structure with *three* other structures in this room.

   You may not talk; this exercise will be done in complete silence.

   You will be given approximately 500 (or fewer for younger kids) cards, and you must use *all* of them.

   Any questions?

3. Throw cards out into the middle of each group.

4. Everybody starts building. After the structures are built, the groups look at their work.

5. For clean up, give instructions in two stages:

   First stage: "Okay, without hurting yourself or anyone else, get those cards off the floor into the air. Go wild!"

   Second stage: "Now it's time to clean up. Put all the cards, stacked neatly, back into the boxes."

Restrictions/Cautions   If there are people with limited mobility, this activity can be adjusted to include them.

Debrief   What was this activity like for you?

Why was it valuable?

What did you need to do in this activity?

What is the lesson?

Author, Author!

Group Cohesion   Low

Target Lessons   Reflective thinking
Critical thinking
Personal worthiness

Materials Needed   Drawing paper
Colored markers or crayons
3 × 5–inch index cards
Masking tape

For the Kids   If you were to title a book about
your life, what would it be?

For the Facilitator   1. Pass out the paper and markers or crayons.

2. Have the kids write a title describing their life as if for an
autobiography. Instruct them to design the book cover,
decorating it with illustrations. They should *not* include their
name on the cover.

3. Post all the book covers on the wall.

4. Instruct each "author" to write three clues about his/her title
on a 3 × 5 card.

5. Collect the index cards, then shuffle and redistribute them
to the group.

6. The group then tries to guess the authors from the clues.

Debrief   Why is this lesson important?

Banners

Group Cohesion   Low

Target Lessons   Positive social orientation

Cooperation

Asking for help

Assertiveness

Close personal relationships, friendships

Materials Needed   A roll of butcher paper

Colored markers or crayons

For the Kids   Symbols are all around us. We talk in symbols and use metaphors to create understanding.

For the Facilitator   Have the kids create a banner using a symbol/metaphor that conjures an image of what they (or the group) believe is important in life. (For example: Life is like a fence. Each picket represents a different aspect of your life.)

Debrief   What is your symbol?

How does the symbol fit your experience?

Alphabet Soup

Group Cohesion   Low

Target Lessons   Problem solving

Data analysis

Team development

Materials Needed   Large index cards (8 × 10–inch), 26 per team

Colored markers (fat ones, so the letters can be
seen at a distance)

A long table (nice but not necessary—the floor
works just as well)

For the Kids   Being on a team requires effort and work. Teams are the foundation
of most things in life. How do you do on a team?

For the Facilitator   1. Divide kids into groups of ten or twelve members. You will need
to divide up younger and older kids so each group has some of
every age (that is, if older kids are the better spellers).

2. Instruct groups to stand single file about ten feet away from any
other team.

3. Each team gets a packet of cards with one letter of the alphabet
written in big letters on each card. They place the cards face up
in a pile in front of them about 35 feet away. A long table or the
floor can accommodate two or three piles.

4. Yell out a word that each team must spell. You will need to prepare a list of four-, five-, six-, and seven-letter words that do not repeat any letter of the alphabet. For example:

Four-letter words	Five-letter words	Six-letter words	Seven-letter words
shop	faith	genius	scraped
love	great	anchor	trailed
hope	grade	around	awoken
team	macho	knight	housing

5. The game (four-letter word variation):

The leader calls out a word.

Four kids from each team run up to the piles of cards.

From their team's pile, each of the four kids grabs a letter that will help spell the word, then runs back to the team.

The team members with the cards must stand in a straight line, facing their other team members, in the proper order to spell the word. (Since everyone is rushing around, it is sometimes a kick to get in the right order.)

The first team to spell the word correctly gets a point.

6. Use a four-letter word to begin the game, then move on to five-, six-, or seven-letter words. Repeat five to seven times.

7. Teams keep track of their own scores.

Restrictions/Cautions   Make sure you use age-appropriate words.

Debrief   What was this activity about?

Why does it teach teamwork?

Who Is This?

Group Cohesion   Low

Target Lessons   Effective communication

Interpersonal sensitivity

Developing an informal support network

Materials Needed   Paper

Pens or pencils

For the Kids   We are going to play a guessing game—about each other.

For the Facilitator   1. Have kids write down three facts about themselves that they don't mind their classmates knowing. Examples may concern hobbies, pets, favorite foods, and so forth.

2. Collect the papers and read them throughout the day, week, or month while the class attempts to guess "Who's this?"

Variations   1. Kids relate funny, embarrassing, or unusual events.

2. Each student gets someone else's card and has until the end of the day (or the next day) to guess "Who's this?"

3. Make cards beforehand, using clues about historical figures, book characters, or anything else that fits into a current lesson.

Debrief   Was it difficult to guess?

What did you find out about yourself? About each other?

Decisions, Decisions

Group Cohesion   Low-Medium

Target Lessons   Positive social orientation

Cooperation

Asking for help

Assertiveness

Developing an informal support network

Reflective thinking

Critical thinking

Materials Needed   Paper

Pens or pencils

For the Kids   Think about all the people and things around you, those who influence the decisions you make.

For the Facilitator   1. Discuss how the people and things around you influence the decisions you make. For example, your friends affect your actions, but so does the neighborhood you live in. Think about what influences your life.

2. Have the kids make lists of the people and things they feel influence them the most. To spur on their thoughts, ask them to think about adults, friends, teachers, music, work, money, love, and so forth.

3. Have the kids rank their selections in order of importance (most important at the top) if they can.

People who influence me	Things that influence me
Adults	1.
1.	2.
2.	3.
Friends	4.
1.	5.
2.	6.

Debrief   Which influences do you wish to change?

Which influences will change as you get older?

What influences your decision about whether to use alcohol or other drugs?

Egghead

Group Cohesion   Low-Medium

Target Lessons   Accepting cultural diversity
Global perspective
Self-evaluation
Personal worthiness
Critical thinking

Materials Needed   Enough eggs so that each person has one
Colored markers (the fine-tipped kind)
A large bowl

For the Kids   Are we all eggheads? What are the similarities between eggs and humans?

For the Facilitator   1. Pass out one white, whole egg (in the shell) to each person.

2. Instruct each person to decorate the egg to look like himself/herself.

3. When decorating is finished, ask everyone to put eggs back into the carton(s).

4. Mix up the cartons. Then pass out the cartons and ask each person to pull out someone else's egg.

5. Ask group members to find the person who matches the egg picked out of the carton and to give the egg back to its creator. Instruct the kids to sit down after they have found the creator of the egg they chose *and* after they have received their original egg back.

6. Let the kids crack their eggs into a large bowl.

Debrief   Why was it so easy to find one another's eggs?

What is the difference between the eggs in the shells and the eggs out of the shells?

Communication 101

Group Cohesion Low-Medium

Target Lessons Effective communication
Effectiveness in work, play, and love
Self-evaluation

Materials Needed Paper
Pens or pencils

For the Kids Communication has occurred only when the receiver of a message understands as you intended him or her to understand.

For the Facilitator
1. Encourage the kids to ask themselves the following questions:

   How well do I get my messages across?

   Do people *hear* what I say?

   How could I improve?

2. Have the kids form groups of six to eight people.

3. Instruct each group to script a play depicting school. The play must demonstrate good, effective communication. Some attitudes or behaviors to demonstrate include the following:

good listener	genuine
caring	respectful
open	helpful

4. Have the groups perform their plays. You can discuss the communication skills being demonstrated as you go along.

Debrief Why is communication so important?

Why's the point of this activity?

Team Totem

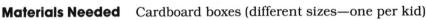

Group Cohesion   Low-Medium

Target Lessons   Accepting cultural diversity

Global perspective

Interpersonal sensitivity

Exhibiting and managing
a range of emotions

Effective communication

Effectiveness in work, play, and love

Materials Needed   Cardboard boxes (different sizes—one per kid)

Paint

Construction paper

Glue

Other miscellaneous art supplies

For the Kids   We are going to make a totem pole about ourselves. Does anyone
know what a totem pole is?

For the Facilitator   1. Divide the kids into teams of four to eight members.

2. Give each team member a cardboard box.

3. Instruct the kids to decorate their boxes with designs that
   have personal meaning (faces and/or symbols). Allow time
   for them to finish.

4. After each kid's box has dried, stack each team's boxes, from
   largest to smallest, to create a totem pole.

5. Have each team share its totem pole with the entire group.

Note   You may want to preface this activity with a discussion of the
cultural uses of totems, especially the function of the totem pole in
Native American culture to represent family lineage and mythical
or historical incidents.

Variation   Have each team create one box, then stack the different
boxes together.

Debrief   What does the box you made say about you?

Mystery!

Group Cohesion   Low-Medium

Target Lessons   Critical thinking

Data analysis

Problem solving

Materials Needed   Prepared clue slips (one set for each group)

For the Kids   Mrs. Butterworth has been murdered. She was a wealthy widow who lived at 1860 Mount Curve Avenue, Rosedale, Maryland, in a sixteen-room house with a live-in maid, cook, and gardener. The cook and the gardener, Mr. and Mrs. Jones, are married. The maid is Ms. Stoltz.

Mrs. Butterworth had three sons. The first two are married and live in Rosedale with their families. John, the eldest, has a wife, Joan, and one daughter, Melissa. Jason, the second son, and his wife, Rebecca, have no children. Dana, the youngest son, is unmarried and goes to school in Boston.

Who killed Mrs. Butterworth? With what? When? Why?

For the Facilitator

1. Divide kids into groups of six to eight members or use a large group of no more than 30 members.

2. Pass out the clues (see pages 143–144): three or four apiece for small groups, one clue apiece for the large group.

3. Explain the rules of the game:

Each statement is a clue.

All groups have the same clues.

Each group must use the clues they have to solve the murder.

Each person holds the clue(s) in his/her hand at all times.

No talking with other groups.

Each group is to find the murderer, the weapon used, the time of the murder, and the motive for the murder. The group is to solve the four parts of the mystery by consensus. When the group solves the murder, one person goes to the leader to give the answer. If the answer is correct, the group will be applauded. If the answer is incorrect, no further specifics will be given.

The Solution Murderer: John Butterworth

Weapon: Gun

Time: 9:00 P.M.

Motive: John's company was failing and he needed money quickly. He and Ms. Stoltz were having an affair. The burglary was meant to throw off the police.

Debrief What were the skills used in this game?

How did the process work?

What did you learn about yourself?

MYSTERY!

The Clues

Several pieces of Mrs. Butterworth's art collection and her jewels were missing.

John was a favorite son.

Dana had been for a walk on the beach and stopped for a beer at a local tavern at 9:00 P.M.

On June 18, Mrs. Butterworth was found dead with a bullet in her chest and a knife wound in her arm.

Ms. Stoltz took Mrs. Butterworth to her bedroom and gave her a sleeping pill.

John arrived at the Butterworth house at 8:50 P.M.

Mr. and Mrs. Jones had been with the Butterworths for 25 years and were rewarded well for their services.

On May 30, Jason and Rebecca left for a three-week European holiday.

John told his wife he had to meet with a customer and left his house at 8:35 P.M.

Ms. Stoltz called John at 8:15 P.M.

When the Joneses returned from town at 9:10 P.M., they met John driving out of the gate.

Dana and his mother argued constantly.

The police found Dana's gun in the bushes behind the house.

A robber carrying a knife had entered the house.

Dana was out of favor with his mother because of his radical ideas.

John was in love with Ms. Stoltz.

Mrs. Butterworth heard a noise in the library at 7:45 P.M. and went to investigate.

Joan was in the process of divorcing John because he was involved with another woman.

143

Mrs. Butterworth was lying on the floor in the library.

Jason had been disinherited because Mrs. Butterworth did not like his wife.

Mr. Jones told police he saw Dana cleaning a pistol in his room on the afternoon of June 18.

The glass in the library door, which opens onto the veranda, was broken.

The robber was caught two days later, but he denied stealing anything.

Dana, home from school for a few weeks, found Mrs. Butterworth's body at 10:30 P.M.

John's company was close to failing, so he was having money problems.

Mrs. Butterworth kept a large collection of jewelry in the house, as well as an art collection valued at half a million dollars.

Mr. and Mrs. Jones had gone to town at 7:30 P.M.

Ms. Stoltz, the maid, had been in the household for five years and was unmarried.

Ms. Stoltz found Mrs. Butterworth in the library at 8:00 P.M. with a cut on her arm.

Safari

Group Cohesion   Medium

Target Lessons   Self-evaluation

Delaying gratification

Future orientation

Problem solving

Decision making

Critical thinking

Healthy expectations and needs

Materials Needed   Camera and film

Paper

Pens or pencils

For the Kids   What does your future hold? Who is in control?

For the Facilitator   1. Have the kids take pictures with a camera of what they want to have in their life at age _____.

2. Explain that taking the steps to meet their goals is like going on a safari. Have them draft a plan to get what they want. The plan should answer these questions:

What steps must you take to get what you want?

What is necessary for you to do?

For example: "I want a 1989 Porsche 911."

How much is it?

How can I pay for it? Cash? A loan?

How do I get a loan?

What do I have to do now?

Is my goal realistic? What changes do I have to make?

3. Have the students create a scrapbook of all the pictures and plans they have created.

Debrief   Are you in control of your life?

Are your goals attainable?

What Do You Think?

Group Cohesion   Medium

Target Lessons   Interpersonal sensitivity

Critical thinking

Decision making

Problem solving

Conflict resolution

Materials Needed   Worksheet 6 (prepared before the activity)

Pens or pencils

For the Facilitator   1. Give each kid a copy of Worksheet 6.

2. Have the kids read the statements, think about each one, and then indicate whether they agree or disagree.

3. Break the kids up into small groups and ask them to discuss their positions with other members of their group.

Variations   The worksheet here is just an example. You can customize your own worksheet using issues relevant to your neighborhood, your school, and the age of your kids.

Debrief   How hard was it to commit to a statement?

What did you learn about yourself?

Were there any surprises?

WORKSHEET 6

Agree   *Disagree*

_____   _____   1. I'd tell the coach if a fellow team member was abusing drugs.

_____   _____   2. I'd rather drink alcohol than be called a chicken.

_____   _____   3. I think marijuana should be legalized.

_____   _____   4. I think all public buildings should be smoke-free.

_____   _____   5. I think people who smoke in nonsmoking areas should be fined.

_____   _____   6. I think the legal drinking age should be 21.

_____   _____   7. I'd report someone who's selling drugs in my school.

_____   _____   8. I think drinking at weekend parties is okay.

_____   _____   9. I'd tell my parents if my brother or sister was abusing alcohol or drugs.

_____   _____   10. I think you can have just as much fun without alcohol or drugs.

Relaxation/Guided Imagery

Group Cohesion   Medium

Target Lessons   Stress management

Using individual talents to personal advantage

Healthy expectations and needs

Reflective thinking

Materials Needed   None

For the Kids   Lie down so that you are not in contact with one another. Recall your successes of today. You'll be using those recollections.

For the Facilitator   1. To begin the relaxation, have the kids lie down and take slow, deep breaths. Tell them to begin to become aware of the things going on around them—sights, sounds, smells, and so forth.

2. As they breathe in and out slowly, gently guide them through each section of their body, starting with their feet and working slowly up the body until you reach the head. Tell them to relax each part as you go.

3. After they are all in a relaxed state of consciousness, guide them to their "special place":

Ask them to visualize a place they've been or would like to visit. Give examples: a flowering meadow, the bottom of the Grand Canyon, a deserted beach, a backyard garden.

Have them visualize this place and themselves in this place. Have them observe the sights and smells and feel any other sensations in their "special place."

Assure them that this is their special place and that it is a safe, wonderful place for them to be.

4. Have them look around their special place for a site to build a "workshop":

   Have them go to this place and begin to visualize how their workshop would look.

   Ask questions: Would you build your workshop from rock, from wood, or from thatch on the beach? Have them build their workshop in their special place where they are safe and all things are wonderful. (Allow time for this. Check whether or not you need to speed up or slow down at this point.)

   Ask them to step back and look at their workshop, in their special place, where they are safe.

   Have them enter their workshop and begin to look around, getting in touch with any sensory data coming in.

   Have them furnish their workshop. Ask questions: Would you have a table? Would you have a couch? What kind? What color? Would you have pictures?

   Let them know this is a safe and wonderful place and that anything is possible.

   Have them sit in their furnished workshop and look around at what they have built and at how they have furnished and decorated their special place. (Continue to reinforce the idea that this is a wonderful place, that they are safe, and that all things are possible in their special workshop.)

5. Bring in a special friend:

   Suggest to the kids that they go to the door to see who's there. When they open the door they realize it is a very special friend—someone they can count on and trust and someone who counts on them and trusts them.

   Have them invite this special person into the workshop to visit. Tell them they can talk if they wish, they can hold hands if they wish, or they can just be together.

   Suggest that this friend is there for support. (Assess the energy again to see where the kids are and to evaluate what type of response you are getting.)

6. Begin to bring the kids back to reality by doing the following:

   Suggest that they now walk their special friend to the door and say good-bye, knowing that at any time they can call this special person back as a resource.

   As the special friend walks out of the workshop—leaving the special place—ask the kids to go outside their workshop, to take a few steps away, and then to turn around and look once again at what they have built.

   Ask them to become aware of what they see, smell, feel, and hear.

Have the students turn away from their workshop, knowing that they can return at any time and that this is a special place that they have built, a secret, safe place where all things are possible.

Have them walk at whatever pace they feel comfortable, following a trail from their special place back to the room.

Have them begin to get back in touch with the sensory stimuli in the room.

7. Reconnect and end:

Ask the kids to sit up.

Let them walk around the room at this point. After a minute or two, ask them to stretch, to roll their heads around gently, and to reconnect with the room.

In the group or in small break-out groups, have them share their experiences.

Variations If the energy level is low, suggest to the kids while they are in the relaxation state that they are recharging their batteries. Tell them to feel the energy entering into their fingertips and toes, filling their bodies with all the energy they need.

Restrictions/Cautions I once attempted this exercise with a group that included several high-risk students and had some difficulty with it. Also, this exercise has limited success with younger kids (twelve, thirteen, and even some fourteen-year-olds). Some kids fall asleep during the exercise, but that does not mean they do not do the guided imagery. Keep this activity light and safe. Avoid any reference to real people who may be in their young lives.

Debrief How did it feel to be in your special place?

What happened?

Were there any surprises?

Bear Traps

Group Cohesion   Medium-High

Target Lessons   Effective communication

Effectiveness in work, play, and love

Positive social orientation

Cooperation

Reflective thinking

Materials Needed   A roll of butcher paper

Colored markers or crayons

For the Kids   What gets in the way of your being the best you can be?

For the Facilitator
1. Have a discussion about the "bear traps" that keep you from communicating and having good relationships with family, friends, teachers, and so on. Here we're talking about the *big* traps: dishonesty, laziness, prejudice.

2. Ask them: "What do you have to do to avoid these bear traps?"

3. Have the kids share their ideas with the group.

4. Have them make a banner representing all of the ideas/things that help avoid bear traps.

Debrief   Are there bear traps in your life?

Who is in control?

Turning It Around

Group Cohesion Medium-High

Target Lessons Critical thinking
Data analysis
Reflective thinking
Conflict resolution
Asking for help
Assertiveness

Materials Needed None

For the Kids You are in charge of how you feel about your life. Taking charge of your life is important for survival.

For the Facilitator 1. Tell the group: Everyone views the world through different experiences. You are in charge. You can *choose* your response.

2. Offer some examples of conflict situations and ask the kids to give you their positive/negative alternatives. (For example: What would you do if a close friend of the past six months pressured you to steal? To engage in sex? To cheat on a test? To take someone's coat?)

Debrief Do you believe you are in control?

What is your evidence?

Do you know folks who are out of control?

Bibliography

Anthony, E. James. "How Children Cope in Families with a Psychotic Parent." In *Infant Psychiatry: A New Synthesis*, eds. E. Rexford et al. New Haven, CT: Yale University Press, 1976.

Anthony, E. James, and Collette Chiland. *The Child in His Family: Vol. 4. Vulnerable Children*. New York: Wiley, 1978.

Anthony, E. James, and Bertram Cohler, eds. *The Invulnerable Child*. New York: Guilford, 1987.

Anthony, E. James, and Cyrille Koupernik, eds. *The Child in His Family: Vol. 3. Children at Psychiatric Risk*. New York: Wiley, 1974.

Benard, Bonnie. *The Case for Peers*. Portland, OR: Western Center for Drug-Free Schools and Communities, 1990.

———. "Peer Programs: The Lodestone to Prevention." *Illinois Prevention Forum* (January 1988).

———. "Protective Factor Research: What We Can Learn from Resilient Children." *Illinois Prevention Forum* (March 1987).

———. "Resiliency Paradigm Validates Craft Knowledge." *Western Center News* (September 1993).

———. "Resiliency Requires Changing Hearts and Minds." *Western Center News* (March 1993).

———. "Towards Family." *Illinois Prevention Forum* (January 1989).

———. "Working Together: Principles of Effective Collaboration." *Illinois Prevention Forum* (October 1989).

———. "Youth Service: From Youth as Problems to Youth as Resources." *Illinois Prevention Forum* (January 1990).

Bennett, William, ed. *American Education: Making It Work*. Washington, DC: U. S. Department of Education, 1988.

Bond, L. A., and J. C. Rosen, eds. *Competence and Coping During Childhood*. Hanover, NH: University of Vermont Press/University Press of New England, 1980.

Bowman, R. P. "Peer Facilitator Programs for Middle Graders: Students Helping Each Other Grow Up." *School Counselor* 33 (January 1986).

Bronfenbrenner, Urie. *The Ecology of Human Development: Experiments by Nature and Design.* Cambridge, MA: Harvard University Press, 1974.

California Department of Education. *Enhancing Opportunities for Higher Education Among Underrepresented Students.* Sacramento: Author, 1990.

Canfield, Jack. *Self-Esteem in the Classroom: A Self-Esteem Curriculum.* Pacific Palisades, CA: Self-Esteem Seminars, 1986.

Carse, James. *Finite and Infinite Games.* New York: Free Press, 1986.

Cowen, Emory et al. "Relationships Between Support and Adjustment Among Children of Divorce." *Journal of Child Psychology and Psychiatry* 31(5), 1990.

Dugan, Timothy, and Robert Coles, eds. *The Child in Our Times.* New York: Brunner-Mazel, 1989.

Elkind, David. *All Grown Up and No Place to Go: Teenagers in Crisis.* Reading, MA: Addison-Wesley, 1984.

———. *The Hurried Child: Growing Up Too Fast Too Soon.* Reading, MA: Addison-Wesley, 1981.

———. "Stress and the Middle Grader." *School Counselor* 33 (January 1986).

Erikson, Erik H. *Childhood and Society.* New York: Norton, 1963.

———. "Identity and the Life Cycle." *Psychological Issues* 1 (January 1959).

Falkenberg, Judy. "Invulnerable Children—How Do They Cope?" *Adamha News* (May 16, 1983).

Fluegelman, Andrew. *More New Games.* New York: Doubleday, 1981.

———. *The New Games Book.* Garden City, NY: Dolphin, 1976.

Garmezy, Norman. "Resiliency and Vulnerability to Adverse Developmental Outcomes Associated with Poverty." *American Behavioral Scientist* (March/April 1991).

———. "Stress-Resistant Children: The Search for Protective Factors." In *Recent Research in Developmental Psychopathology,* ed. J. E. Stevenson. Oxford: Pergamon, 1985.

Garmezy, Norman et al. "The Study of Stress and Competence in Children: A Building Block for Developmental Psychopathology." *Child Development* 55 (1984).

Garmezy, Norman, and Michael Rutter. *Stress, Coping and Development in Children.* New York: McGraw-Hill, 1983.

Gibbs, Jeanne, and Sherrin Bennett. *Together We Can: A Framework for Community Prevention Planning.* Seattle: Comprehensive Health Education Foundation, 1990.

Glasser, William. *The Quality School: Managing Students Without Coercion.* New York: Harper & Row, 1990.

———. *Reality Therapy.* New York: Harper & Row, 1969.

———. *Schools Without Failure.* New York: Harper & Row, 1969.

Glenn, H. Stephen, and Jane Nelsen. *Raising Self-Reliant Children in a Self-Indulgent World.* Rocklin, CA: Prima, 1989.

Good, Thomas L., and Jere E. Brophy. *Looking in Classrooms.* New York: Harper & Row, 1984.

Goodlad, John. *A Place Called School: Prospects for the Future.* New York: McGraw-Hill, 1984.

Haggerty, Robert J. Foreword to *Stress, Coping and Development in Children,* eds. Norman Garmezy and Michael Rutter. New York: McGraw-Hill, 1983.

Hawkins, J. D. et al. "Childhood Predictors of Adolescent Substance Abuse: Toward an Empirically Grounded Theory." *Journal of Children in Contemporary Society* 18 (1985).

Haynes, Marion. *Effective Meeting Skills: A Practical Guide for More Productive Meetings.* Menlo Park, CA: Crisp Publications, 1988.

Janis, Irving, and Leon Mann. *Decision Making: A Psychological Analysis of Conflict, Choice, and Commitment.* New York: Free Press, 1979.

Johnson, Vern. *I'll Quit Tomorrow.* New York: HarperCollins, 1980.

Lazarus, Richard, and Susan Folkman. *Stress, Appraisal, and Coping.* New York: Springer, 1984.

Lazarus, Richard et al. "Stress and Adaptational Outcomes: The Problem of Confounded Measures." *American Psychologist* 40 (July 1985).

Lefkowitz, Bernard. *Tough Change: Growing Up on Your Own in America.* New York: Free Press, 1987.

Levin, Pamela, ed. *Educational Reform for Disadvantaged Students: An Emerging Crisis* (NEA Search). Washington, DC: National Education Association, 1986.

Meisels, Samuel, and Jack Shonkoff, eds. *Handbook of Early Childhood Intervention.* New York: Cambridge University Press, 1990.

Murphy, Lois, and Alice Moriarty. *Vulnerability, Coping and Growth: From Infancy to Adolescence.* New Haven, CT: Yale University Press, 1976.

A Nation Prepared: Teachers for the 21st Century. Washington, DC: Carnegie Forum on Education and the Economy, 1986.

Orlick, Terry. *The Cooperative Sports and Games Book*. New York: Pantheon, 1978.

Piaget, Jean, and Barbel Inhelder. *The Psychology of the Child*, trans. Helen Weaver. New York: Basic, 1969.

Presseisen, Barbara. "Teaching Thinking and At-Risk Students: Defining a Population." In *At-Risk Students: Perspectives from Research*. Washington, DC: National Education Association, 1988.

Rice, Wayne, and Mike Yaconelli. *Play It: Great Games for Groups*. Grand Rapids, MI: Zondervan, 1986.

Riddy, W. Brandon, and Kaleel Jamison. *Team Building: Blueprints for Productivity and Satisfaction*. Alexandria, VA: NTL Institute for Applied Behavioral Science, 1988.

Rutter, Michael. *Changing Youth in a Changing Society*. Cambridge, MA: Harvard University Press, 1979.

———. *Helping Troubled Children*. New York: Plenum, 1975.

———. "Protective Factors in Children's Responses to Stress and Disadvantage." In *Primary Prevention of Psychopathology: Social Competence in Children* (Vol. 3), eds. M. W. Kent and J. E. Rolf. Hanover, NH: University Press of New England, 1979.

———. "Resilience in the Face of Adversity: Protective Factors and Resistance to Psychiatric Disorder." *British Journal of Psychiatry* 147 (1985).

———. "Resilient Children," *Psychology Today* (March 1984).

———. "Stress, Coping, and Development: Some Issues and Some Questions." *Journal of Child Psychology and Psychiatry* 22 (April 1981).

Rutter, Michael et al. *Fifteen Thousand Hours*. Cambridge, MA: Harvard University Press, 1979.

Segal, Julius. *Winning Life's Toughest Battles: Roots of Human Resilience*. New York: Ballantine, 1987.

Seligman, Martin. *Learned Optimism*. New York: Knopf, 1990.

Selye, Hans. "History and Present Status of the Stress Concept." In *Handbook of Stress: Theoretical and Clinical Aspects*, eds. Leo Goldberger and Shlomo Breznitz. New York: Free Press, 1982.

Slavin, Robert et al. *Effective Programs for Students at Risk*. Needham Heights, MD: Allyn and Bacon, 1989.

Stoddard, Lynn. *Redesigning Education: A Guide for Developing Human Greatness*. Tucson, AZ: Zephyr, 1992.

Tobin, L. *What to Do with a Child Like This? Inside the Lives of Troubled Children*. Duluth, MN: Whole Person Associates, 1991.

Wallerstein, Judith, and Joan Kelly. *Surviving the Breakup: How Children and Parents Cope with Divorce*. New York: Basic, 1980.

Wehlage, Gary, ed. *Reducing the Risk: Schools as Communities of Support*. Philadelphia: Falmer Press, 1989.

Werner, Emmy E. "High-Risk Children in Young Adulthood: A Longitudinal Study from Birth to 32 Years." *American Journal of Orthopsychiatry* 59 (1989).

———. "Resilient Children." In *Annual Editions: Human Development,* eds. H. E. Fitzgerald and M. G. Walraven. Sluice Dock, CT: Dushkin, 1986.

Werner, Emmy E., and Ruth S. Smith. *Vulnerable but Invincible: A Longitudinal Study of Resilient Children and Youth*. New York: Adams, Bannister, and Cox, 1989.

Wine, Jeri, and Marti Syme, eds. *Social Competence*. New York: Guilford, 1981.

Zigler, Edward et al. *Children, Families, and Government: Perspectives on American Social Policy*. New York: Cambridge University Press, 1983.

Index of Activities

About the Author

MICHELLE KARNS IS A CHARISMATIC LEADER for educational change. Her passion is to help schools, communities, and families create caring environments that foster healthy life-styles and student success. She has traveled extensively throughout the United States pleading for greater understanding of children and suggesting ways that this may be accomplished.

Her many keynote addresses and conference presentations have focused on increasing audience awareness of the reality experienced by today's children and on ways to build individual coping skills. She does this in two ways: by reaching adults who have influence with kids and by interacting with kids directly. She originated the popular Kids Day program, now operating in more than a thousand schools, and has helped develop other programs that engender healthy relationships among kids, parents, and teachers.

In the school systems where she has worked as a National Training Associates trainer, Michelle Karns has been a catalyst for change. All of Michelle's work reflects her commitment to making real the dream of kid-centered, community-supported, healthy school environments. With parents she strives for more empathetic parent-child relationships. With school staffs she strives for greater resiliency building and more kid-centered activities within the classroom. With kids she strives to promote prosocial thoughtfulness and intergroup acceptance.

Michelle Karns has a bachelor's degree from Fort Wright College in Spokane, Washington, and both a master's degree in public administration and a certificate in alcohol studies from Seattle University. She has worked as a therapist, a teacher, a trainer, and a writer. She currently resides in Davis, California, with her husband, Robert, and her daughter, Katy.

About
National Training
Associates

NATIONAL TRAINING ASSOCIATES (NTA) is a training and consultation firm comprised of educational specialists who serve as organizational catalysts. The consultants are dedicated to the goal of encouraging the personal, organizational, and social change that fosters generational wellness for children, families, organizations, and communities.

Since 1982 NTA has been providing training and consultation services to assist schools in planning, organizing, implementing, and evaluating comprehensive student assistance programs. From their genesis in drug/alcohol identification and intervention to their current emphasis on community-based planning and school restructuring, NTA is continually evolving their approach to meet the ever-changing needs of schools and the communities they serve.

One aspect that has remained constant is NTA's commitment to a team approach. Over the past twelve years, the team concept has expanded to include students, parents, community agencies, and community and business members. YES (Youth Empowering Systems) is the name given to NTA's team approach within schools, and its foundation is the development and maintenance of the student assistance program.

In the YES trainings, NTA helps educators design a program that promotes general wellness and encourages school personnel to become aware sooner of students experiencing personal distress. Building resiliency and enhancing protective factors are key ingredients in this empowerment process. Program graduates report a sense of renewed dedication to the task of helping young people, a belief that change is possible, and a feeling of hope for the future. As a result of NTA's trainings in rural and urban areas throughout the United States, more than 2,000 campuses are providing effective prevention and intervention programs for students.

NTA offers a comprehensive consultation and training program, like the YES program for schools, to community agencies and businesses. Building Community Partnerships is designed to help "whole system" teams develop and implement community-based plans that include community planning, economic development, job training, mentoring, violence prevention, and programs for youth.

Additional NTA programs include the following:

Building Rapport with High-Risk Youth

Building Student Resiliency

Nonverbal Strategies for Classroom Management (ENVoY)

Mentor Training

Peer Mediation and Conflict Management

Support Group Training

Kids Empowering Day

Building Parent Involvement

Student Leadership and Responsibility

Facilitating High Performance Meetings and Teams

Team Building

Strategic Planning

School Restructuring

Site-Based Management and Decision Making

Developing Leadership Potential

Trainer Presentation Skills

Community/School Safety and Violence Prevention

Aggression Replacement Training

For more information regarding NTA and their trainings and services, call or write:

National Training Associates
P. O. Box 1270
Sebastopol, CA 95473
(800) 624–1120 from outside California
(707) 829–1884 from inside California